GROWTH GROUPS

GROWTH GROUPS

**Marriage and Family Enrichment
Creative Singlehood • Human Liberation
Youth Work • Social Change**

Howard Clinebell

Abingdon
Nashville

GROWTH GROUPS

Marriage and Family Enrichment, Creative Singlehood, Human
Liberation, Youth Work, Social Change
Originally published as *The People Dynamic*

Copyright © 1972 by Howard J. Clinebell, Jr.
1977 edition by Abingdon

Library of Congress Cataloging Number: 77-80169

ISBN 0-687-15975-X

MANUFACTURED BY THE PARTHENON PRESS AT
NASHVILLE, TENNESSEE, UNITED STATES OF AMERICA

Contents

The highest expression of civilization is not its art but the supreme tenderness that people are strong enough to feel and show toward one another. . . . If our civilization is breaking down, as it appears to be, it is not because we lack the brainpower to meet its demands but because our feelings are being dulled. What our society needs is a massive and pervasive experience of resensitization.

NORMAN COUSINS
(*Saturday Review*, January 23, 1971)

Caring deeply for others is now as necessary as food, air and water . . . not through duty, but joy. . . . The impulse toward delight can energize every educational, religious and social enterprise. . . . A deeply feeling person, tuned to mankind's common wavelength, can't hurt other people, poison the Planet, destroy what is beautiful. . . . It's a good time to start crossing boundaries. Take a chance.

GEORGE B. LEONARD
(*Look*, January 13, 1970)

A Preview

"What surprised me was how much I have going *for* me . . . There's a lot more of me than I ever let myself be."

"I'm able to feel and like my own strength as a human being . . . I'm doing a lot less of this god-making of authority people."

"The thing that helped most was discovering that I can be *both* loving and honest—that I don't have to play the phony games that keep people a mile away."

"This group has helped us talk about the things that hurt and the things we both really care about. We've gotten connected again!"

"It hit me that the group liked me as me! Without all the strings that I've attached to liking me."

THESE STATEMENTS, made during evaluation sessions, suggest the kinds of changes people undergo in growth groups. Not everyone has a dramatic awakening. Many experience more gradual growth. Some find group sessions unproductive and disappointing. Much depends on the particular group, its leader, and the individual's readiness for growth.

But, all things considered, *growth groups seem to be the most effective means for the maximum number of persons to experience enlivening within themselves and in their relationships with others!* These groups offer a workable method by which "normal" people can break out of their boxes, discover unused strengths and deepen their intimate relationships. Growth groups are described in these pages with enthusiasm born of frequent amazement at their positive influence on others and with gratitude for the help these groups have provided in my own struggle to keep growing. My enthusiasm is tempered by a realistic appraisal of the problems and risks in any activity involving people and their relationships. I recommend growth groups, not as a magic solution to every problem, but as a practical method of helping people develop their unused strengths and abilities.

In the small, sharing group lies the power which enables persons to love more fully and live more creatively. This is the *people dynamic—the power we have to recreate each other and ourselves through caring and sharing.* Growth groups offer a means of releasing the people dynamic to help humanize personal relationships and to help create a world in which every person will have the opportunity to develop his full, unique capacities.

What this book offers is not a real package nor a complete design. It presents ideas and methods with which I continue to experiment and struggle. My hope is that it will prove useful to participants in growth groups; to professionals (clergymen, teachers, youth workers, and school counselors,) who lead small groups as one part of their jobs; to counselors and psychotherapists who desire to give stronger emphasis to the growth approach in their groups; and to nonprofessionals who are in training to lead growth groups.

Many of us in the person-centered professions are discouraged with the results of present methods. We know there's something wrong with teaching in our schools when so many students learn only a fraction of what they could. Something must be lacking in our church services and programs when a high proportion of members find religion dull, if not empty. And something is surely wrong with our social agencies when a high percentage of clients find little or no help with their problems. I know the feelings of discouragement. I also know from experience that professional renewal can occur. Growth groups (in and out of the classroom) constitute the most energizing and change-producing aspect of my work. The experience of the last five years and a decade of experimenting with small groups before that have convinced me that growth groups are on the cutting edge in counseling, education, and community-building.

If you've never tried a growth group, this book will have much more meaning if you join one and meet the people dynamic firsthand. Locating a growth-oriented group with a competent leader, near at hand and within your financial limitations, may not be easy. Check with a knowledgeable clergyman, or the local mental health or family service agencies. Many churches have growth groups open to nonmembers. Organizations such as the "Y" and the local Family Service Association agencies often sponsor growth-oriented groups. In colleges, small groups are often sponsored ecumenically at student religious centers.

If no small group exists which matches your needs, why not start one? Find a few friends with similar needs and line up a well-trained leader by contacting a counselor, clergyman, or agency. A modest contribution per person will suffice to pay the leader a professional fee for his services. Or you might start by inviting a small group you're already in (church, school class, club, youth group, professional association, etc.) to read and discuss this book. During the discussion you can decide together whether and how to develop a group for those who desire it.

My thanks to those friends and colleagues who shared with me their varied experiences with small groups, thereby enriching the ideas and examples presented in this book; to Leonard Munter who advised me on the application of the growth-groups concept to schools; to Charles Rassieur for his work on references and on the index; and to my wife, Charlotte, for her insights and collaboration, particularly on the use of groups in women's liberation, with children, and in agency settings.

During the struggles to organize and articulate these ideas, my thoughts have returned often to the group experiences in which—over the years—the ideas were germinated; I remember with warm gratitude the friends and fellow searchers with whom I experienced the people dynamic—the *transforming power of loving people*. My wish for you, the reader, is that this book may lead you to group experiences in which you'll discover new dimensions of this power.

HOWARD J. CLINEBELL,

Claremont, California

GROWTH
GROUPS

CHAPTER 1

Growth Groups—Key to Aliveness

The aim of life is to be fully born, though its tragedy is that most of us die before we are thus born. To live is to be born every moment. . . . Death occurs when birth stops. . . . The answer is to develop one's awareness, one's reason, one's capacity to love, to such a point that one transcends one's own egocentric involvement, and arrives at a new harmony, at a new oneness with the world.

ERICH FROMM, "Zen Buddhism and Psychoanalysis"[1]

THE EVERESTLIKE ISSUE that now towers over mankind is *life*—its quality, perhaps even its survival. The perspective of moon flights has sharpened our awareness that our spaceship "earth" is a small, precious oasis of life in the vast, frigid void of cosmic space. Can we make it a place where life can flourish for all our fellow passengers? A place where the possibilities of a fully developed life will not be crushed for millions by poverty, disease, injustice, violence, ignorance, and despair?

In our *nations and communities*, the quality of life is the imperative issue. Can we learn to love and respect the natural world? Can we stop poisoning ourselves by contaminating our air, our rivers, our oceans? Can we stop squandering our nat-

1

ural resources and give thought to the quality of life for our children and our children's children? Can we make our social environment—especially our deteriorating inner cities—places of life and growth, rather than misery and despair?

The quality of life is also the issue in our *institutions*; lightning-fast social change has made many of these ineffective in meeting contemporary human needs. How can more. of our schools make education a continuing adventure of the mind? How can we help more people on job treadmills find fulfillment in their work? How can our churches make religion what it should be— an experience of liberation, healing, and fulfillment of the spirit? How can we awaken the joy, the lift, the celebration?

The quality of life is also the issue in our *family relations*. Many of us are "successful" in all areas of our lives except those that count most—our intimate relationships. Can we make our homes function more as the growth-centers they should be and less as the factories for programming conformity, which they often are? In marriage, the most promising area for mutual growth, too few of us learn to find fulfillment. We live alone together, settling for half-marriages or less.

The quality of life is very much an issue in our *individual worlds*. Gallup pollsters asked a cross-section of Americans whether they experience life as dull and routine, or as exciting. *Fifty-one percent said their lives were dull and routine!* Among people over 50, 60 percent find life dull.[2] Psychologists have declared that most of us use only a small fraction of our brain-power, our creativeness, our personality potential. What a waste of our most precious gift!

I was made aware of this during a recent backpack trip down into the Grand Canyon. A ranger-naturalist, discussing the geology of that magnificent chasm, pointed out that each step down took the hiker back *30,000 years* in geological time. As we descended to Bright Angel Creek near the Colorado, I was suddenly confronted with the fact of the brevity and fragility of human life—my own and that of those I love. I was forced to ask myself some painful questions: how am I using my brief days on the earth? am I treating life—my own and others'—as the precious thing it is?

WHAT IS A GROWTH GROUP?

How does all this relate to growth groups? Life can flourish on our planet, among nations, and in our cities and institutions, only if we say "Yes!" to the life within us. Growth groups are instruments for *enlivening* individuals and relationships. They're *human potentials groups,* designed to help us discover and use more of our latent resources.

As used herein, the term "growth group" is any group, whatever its name, with three characteristics: (1) A dominant (though not exclusive) purpose is the personal growth of participants—emotionally, interpersonally, intellectually, spiritually. (2) A growth-facilitating style of leadership is used—first by the designated leader and gradually by the entire group so that the group itself becomes an instrument of growth. (3) The growth-orientation is the guiding perspective; the emphasis is more on unused potential, here-and-now effectiveness in living, and future goals—than on past failures, problems, and pathology.

To be maximally effective, a growth group should have these additional characteristics: (4) The group is composed of relatively functional people so that its aim is "making well people better."[3] (5) It is small enough to allow group trust and depth relationships to develop. (6) There is a two-way movement from personal feelings to relevant content, i.e., it blends group counseling and person-centered education. (7) Applying learning from group experiences to relationships outside the group is encouraged as an essential part of personal growth. (8) The group encourages constructive changes in both attitudes and feelings on the one hand, and in behavior and relationships on the other.[4]

The growth-orientation—in contrast to the sickness-orientation which has characterized classical psychotherapy and most group therapy—is a distinct way of viewing people and the helping process. For example, in marriage *growth* groups, issues such as these are emphasized: What do you *like* about each other and your relationship? How can you *build* on these things? What kind of marriage do you *want* to have in six months? What do you need to start *doing* now to move toward that? The focus of traditional therapy—on negative feelings, accumulated hurts and frustrations, patterns of relating to the past—are not ignored,* but they are always balanced by the positive growth emphasis.

In contrast to the pathology orientation, the growth approach elicits different responses from people, draws on different sides of their personalities (the healthy sides), and suggests that help lies in a different direction—setting goals and working toward them rather than striving mainly to repair damaged areas of relationships and personalities.

When a person learns to use his latent resources, it often becomes unnecessary to deal in depth with his "pathology." He may become a more effective person without having to cope extensively with his hangups from the past. Viable hopes and plans for the future can *pull* a person as insistently as his past *pushes* him. In growth groups, the growth-perspective is central. It functions like a pair of eyeglasses, permitting leader and group members to see each other in terms of what they can become. This is a liberating perception.

A person whose growth has been frozen for years (as indicated by rigid, neurotic, or disturbed behavior) often cannot respond to an unmodified growth approach until psychotherapy frees him to

* Growth often occurs as one—by choosing to live in the present—breaks the tyranny which the past has been allowed to wield over one's life.

use everyday relationships and groups to nurture his growth. The most effective forms of therapy today focus on both healing and growth.

Unlike most therapy groups, growth groups often use "head-level input"—the study of a selection or brief statement on adolescent psychology, for example, as a kickoff for a parents' session on youth. In contrast to the procedure of most "study groups," the content is dealt with on a *personal* level, in terms of the feelings, struggles, hopes, and goals of the members. The content is chosen to stimulate interaction or to fill explicit needs of members. Unlike therapy groups, growth groups may have task- as well as growth-goals—e.g., social action or women's liberation groups. The task is valuable in itself, but it is also used as an opportunity for growth. Because the growth group setup aims at increasing coping skills as well as awakening persons to themselves, it can be adapted to many task goals.

A good growth group aims at a balanced emphasis on the three interdependent dimensions of human development—*inreach, outreach,* and *upreach.* Inreach refers to growth in awareness—coming alive to oneself. The walls between us are extensions of the walls within us. Inreach means relating responsibly and responsively to oneself—taking one's own feelings and needs seriously. Outreach means relating responsibly and responsively to others. It involves developing a life-style of "generativity"—psychoanalyst Erik Erikson's apt term for generating life in the ongoing stream of society—living in terms of the growth needs of the family of man. Upreach refers to growth of a stronger, more trustful connection with the *vertical* dimension—with the Source of all life and growth. Attention to upreach growth is just as vital in a school or secular group as in church or temple. Vertical issues are not just the concern of churches. They are the profoundly human issues that face us all.

THE DIRECTIONS OF GROWTH

The guiding purpose of growth groups, as we have seen, is to *enhance the quality of life*—to help each participant (member or leader) become more fully alive.

I am alive to the degree that I am—	*I am dead to the degree that I am—*
Aware: in touch with my feelings and with my body.	Out of touch with myself.
Relating (communicating) with others in depth.	Living in the solitary confinement of a world of walls.
Authentic: open and congruent. Owning myself.	Phony: hidden, playing a cover-up role.
Loving: spontaneously caring and giving myself in relationships.	Manipulating: defensively controlling for egocentric ends.
Enjoying: pleasuring, playing, celebrating life.	Plodding: caught in the rat race I have created.
Spontaneous: free to experience and to choose.	Compulsive: programmed, driven by the oughts and the shoulds.
Creating: making or doing something satisfying and/or significant.	Vegetating: treadmilling.
Risking: adventuring.	Playing it safe: living in my box.
Present in the here-and-now, enriched by past/future.	Existing in memories and future fantasies; not present.
Coping responsibly with circumstances.	Being "lived" by circumstances; blaming, projecting responsibility.
Connected with the Source—nature, the human race, God.	Isolated—"an orphan in the universe."
Growing toward using more of my potentialities.	Stagnating or regressing in the use of my gifts.

Summarizing these goals, a growth group provides an interpersonal environment in which persons can become more *aware, re-*

lating, authentic, loving, enjoying, spontaneous, creating, risking, present, coping, and connected with the Source. It is in this process of fulfilling one's potential for full aliveness that one experiences inner affirmation and joy.

Growth groups aim at helping each person discover and move along his own unique road. Within an atmosphere that values aliveness and lets it flower, the individual finds growth directions which are in some ways as unique as his fingerprints. But human needs are similar enough that group members usually empathize with each other's goals. The young man who declared passionately, "I want to stop plodding and fly for a change!" found the whole group resonating to his aspirations.

In a frequently reprinted article, "Are You Alive?"[5] Stuart Chase distinguished between "living" and "existing." He was living, he says, when he experienced love, friendship, danger, play, laughter, art, food when hungry, sleep when tired, the mountains, sea, and stars. In contrast, he only existed when his lot was drudgery, or attending social functions, or experiencing ugliness and monotony. Of the 168 hours in the previous week, he found that he had lived only 40 of them. How about the past week in your life? The purpose of growth groups is to improve the ratio on the side of living.

HOW DOES GROWTH OCCUR?

Knowing how growth occurs can help one facilitate the process in a group:

Everyone has within him an impulse to develop his potentialities. This drive is our fundamental resource in education, counseling, and growth groups. The teacher's, counselor's, and group leader's most indispensable skill is his ability to awaken this drive. Some people have squelched the growth urge for so long that they're oblivious to it. The drive continues to express itself, however, in vague restlessness, in general apathy, or in the guilt/

depression/anger syndrome that results from dammed-up growth.

The growth drive is stimulated or blocked by the quality of relationships. Growth occurs in a relationship in which there is mutual feeding of the basic heart-hungers—the hunger for love, affirmation, freedom, pleasure, adventure, meaning. Shallow, manipulative relating (which is all that many people do), blocks growth and damages self-esteem. If such I-it relationships dominate one's early life, the growth drive becomes encrusted in defensiveness and fear; resistance to growth becomes intense. Growth-stimulating relationships are warm, caring, and trustful at the same time that they are honest, confronting, and open. *Caring + confrontation = growth!* This is the growth formula.

Growth is an inner fulfillment and unfolding. Growth-producing relationships nurture and release an inner process; manipulation or attempts to coerce the person to change do not produce growth. The patterns and direction of growth reflect the person's individuality. Growth results from discovering, affirming, and rejoicing in who one truly is, rather than pursuing an idealized image of what one should be. Becoming takes place by being.

Growth is an experience of the whole person in many areas*— feelings, behavior, attitudes, relationships. Changes in any area often trigger changes in other areas. By choosing to use your present freedom to relate to others more authentically and responsibly, you enhance your self-esteem. By choosing to be true to yourself now, you help create your future.

The small sharing group is the ideal arena for deepening relationships and consequently accelerating growth. To continue growing, every person requires a depth relationship with at least one other human being. A small network of depth relationships is even better. The group is an interpersonal laboratory for testing and learning better ways of relating. It provides a place to do one's

---

* Growth groups function at various levels, depending on the goals and the leadership.

"growth work"—that essential struggle to let go of costly but comfortable defenses against growth—and to find and own oneself.

Small group methods are most effective with relatively whole people whose growth impulses are active and accessible. These are people who, in Abraham Maslow's terms, are motivated at least as strongly by self-actualization trends (the need to grow) as by deficiency needs (the hunger for security, respect, love, etc.).[6] Those with intense deficiency needs require therapy; those with a predominance of self-actualization needs respond to growth-oriented methods. The pain of deficiency needs provides the *push* of therapy; the *pull* of self-actualization tendencies is a major motivation for growth. Relatively healthy people have sufficiently gratified their basic needs so that their self-actualization or growth drives can function freely.* Growth-motivated people experience growth, in itself, as a rewarding, exciting process.

The growth-facilitating style of leadership can be learned by anyone who is relatively open with himself and others—or is willing to undergo the therapeutic and growth experiences to become so.

Institutions become viable to the degree that they provide opportunities for human growth and fulfillment. Renewal in churches, schools, and agencies will occur only as they become human development centers!

A PLAN FOR A GROWTH-ORIENTED COMMUNITY

Developing well-led, inexpensive, and accessible groups is a high priority goal for our communities. Visualize a city with a network of growth groups in each neighborhood available to people of all ages and sponsored by schools, churches, and community agencies as well as corporations, unions, professional associations, and fraternal groups. Perhaps neighborhood organiza-

---

* There are times when all of us experience intense deficiency needs and other times when our growth needs may be dominant. In some persons, one or the other is dominant most of the time.

tions could also sponsor groups for their members. In such a growth-oriented community, the people dynamic would be taken seriously and the wealth of previously unused human potential would contribute to improving the quality of life in that community.

In every community there are hundreds of ordinary, functioning people who—when they let themselves feel—long to experience more vividly, relate more pleasurably, and work more effectively. Some will meet their needs by going to Esalen-type growth centers. But the vast majority will not, because such centers seem too expensive, too distant, too exotic. Growth groups in local communities could provide a periodic "growth boost" to enhance living and relating for these relatively healthy persons.

The basic resources for developing community growth networks already exist. Hundreds of educators, clergymen, and counselors are already experimenting with growth-oriented groups, and many others are eager to find group approaches for releasing human potential. Some 100 or more growth institutes operate in North America, and many colleges and seminaries now provide training in group methods. How rapidly growth-oriented communities develop depends, to a considerable extent, on people like you. If you see growth groups as a means of improving life for people in your organization or community, join one or use your influence to help launch new groups with well-trained leaders. Or, if you have the inclination and aptitudes, obtain the necessary training to lead groups yourself. In short, become a "committee of one" dedicated to the fullest possible use of the people dynamic in your community.

VARIETIES OF GROWTH GROUPS

The versatility and adaptability of the growth group approach can be suggested by listing some of the types of groups which have proved to be productive; groups such as these could be included in a community's growth network:

Youth groups to work through unfinished personal identity.

Preparation for marriage groups.

"Keeping Our Marriage Growing" groups (recently married).

Marriage enrichment groups for parents of young children; for parents of adolescents (middle marrieds); and for empty nest marriages.

"Making the Most of Maturity" groups (over-40 groups).

Groups for singles.

Play groups for normal children.

Parent-child and parent-youth dialogue groups.

Preparation for childbirth, leaving home, retirement (and other developmental crises) groups.

Study-growth groups with a dual focus on intellectual and interpersonal growth (often centering on a book).

Liberation groups for women, for men, and for couples desiring fresh approaches to male/female roles.

Creativity groups using drama, poetry, painting, pottery, body movement (creative dance), yoga, etc. as a stimulus to growth.

Groups for coping constructively with common causes of stress—e.g., aging parents, physical handicaps, a handicapped child, "'adolescing" children.

Action-growth groups with a dual focus on personal development and training for some significant task.

Spiritual growth groups aimed primarily at group interaction around meaning, values, and other religious growth issues.

Ecology groups for tuning in on nature and saving the environment.

Multiple-family groups (including communes).

Growth groups for the divorced.

Bereavement recovery groups.

Youth groups searching for nondrug ways of turning on.

Career development groups.

Follow-up groups for persons released from mental and correctional institutions.

Stage two groups for those who have found help in psychotherapy or self-help programs like Alcoholics Anonymous, Alanon, etc.

This list is only suggestive. The possible applications of the growth-group approach are limited only by the imagination and leadership resources available.

THE POWER OF GROWTH

While reflecting on why the people dynamic which one encounters in small groups has such power, I came upon a moving passage from Loren Eiseley. In it he discusses the amazing development of man's brain which, in a relatively brief time (anthropologically speaking), allowed him to emerge from animalism to self-awareness:

It was truly man who, walking memoryless through bars of sunlight and shade in the morning of the world, sat down and passed a wondering hand across his heavy forehead. Time and darkness, knowledge of good and evil have walked with him ever since. . . . A new world of terror and loneliness appears to have been created in the soul of man.

For the first time in four billion years, a living creature had contemplated himself and heard with a sudden unaccountable loneliness, the whisper in the night reeds. Perhaps he knew, there in the grass by the chill waters, that he had before him an immense journey.[7]

Perhaps it is this self-awareness, this existential loneliness, this sense of the vastness of the universe and our fragile place in it, that make all of us long for comrades to share the immense journey. Perhaps these considerations are at the roots of the will to relate; perhaps they account for the power of the people dynamic in our lives.

THE TIME IS NOW!

There is a special urgency about providing an enlarging network of varied growth opportunities. The pressures of massive loneliness, love-hunger, and diminished self-esteem already stand at explosive levels. In shallow, fleeting, manipulative, I-it relating there's nothing to replenish that most indispensable of inner resources, *self-esteem.* Consider the lethal implications of masses of humanity, filled with anger bred in loneliness and armed with technology's weapons for mutual destruction. The stakes are high!

The *will to relate* is the most powerful of human strivings. Only in and through relationships can we become pro-life people and work effectively for a society that supports human fulfillment. Growth groups constitute one important answer to this basic need. They provide opportunities to learn the interpersonal skills which alone can produce what we want—better relationships, healthier personalities for our children, more fulfilling vocations and better communities—in short, a more humanizing world.

In *The Greening of America* Charles Reich describes the profound changes now occurring in human consciousness:

There is a revolution coming. It will not be like revolutions of the past. It will originate with the individual and with culture. . . . It is now spreading with amazing rapidity. . . . It promises a higher reason, a more human community, a new and liberated individual. Its ultimate creation will be a new enduring wholeness and beauty—a renewed relationship of man to himself, to other men, to society, to nature, and to the land.[8]

Reich's "Consciousness III" is characterized by the rediscovery of the self, genuine spontaneity, new relationships, the rebirth of celebration. These are precisely the kinds of changes which occur in growth groups.

There are some risks in growth groups. But the dangers and

loss to society of *not* releasing the wealth of untapped human possibilities, make these risks seem small by comparison. Growth groups can help make the power of authentic relationships—the people dynamic—a liberating experience in community after community for *the greening of the world.* The time is now! The world won't wait! So let's do the thinking, strategizing and creative experimentation with small groups that is needed to develop islands of caring and growth in every part of the lonely sea which is our world.

Additional Reading—Small Groups

These books are related to the issues and topics of Chapters 1-3.
("L" = of interest primarily to group leaders. Others of general interest.)

L   Burton, Arthur (Ed.), *Encounter, The Theory and Practice of Encounter Groups.* San Francisco: Jossey-Bass, 1970.

Gardner, John W., *Self-Renewal.* New York: Harper Colophon Books, 1964.

L   Goldberg, Carl, *Encounter: Group Sensitivity Training Experience.* New York: Science House, 1970.

L   Kemp, C. Gratton, *Small Groups and Self-Renewal.* New York: The Seabury Press, 1971.

Maslow, Abraham H., *Toward a Psychology of Being.* Princeton: D. Van Nostrand, 1962.

Maslow, Abraham H., *Motivation and Personality,* 2nd ed. New York: Harper & Row, 1970.

Murphy, Gardner, *Human Potentialities.* New York: Basic Books, 1961.

L   Ohlsen, Merle M., *Group Counseling.* New York: Holt, Rinehart and Winston, 1970.

Olmsted, Michael S., *The Small Group.* New York: Random House, 1959.

Otto, Herbert A., *Group Methods Designed to Actualize Human Potentials.* Chicago: Achievement Motivation Systems, 1967.

Rogers, Carl R., *Carl Rogers on Encounter Groups.* New York: Harper & Row, 1970.

L   Ruitenbeek, H.M. (Ed.) *Group Therapy Today* New York: Atherton Press, 1969.

REFERENCES

1. D. T. Suzuki, Erich Fromm, and Richard DeMartino, *Zen Buddhism and Psychoanalysis* (New York: Harper & Row, 1960), pp. 87-88.

2. Gallup Poll, *Los Angeles Times,* October 6, 1969, Part I, p. 34.

3. William C. Schutz, *Joy, Expanding Human Awareness* (New York: Grove Press, 1967), p. 10.

4. The term "encounter group" refers to one type of growth group. I prefer "growth group" because this term describes the purpose and orientation of the group, rather than a primary means—encountering—by which it is achieved. "Growth group," as used herein, includes more types of groups than usually covered by the term "encounter group."

5. First appearance, *The Nation,* 1922.

6. Abraham Maslow, *Toward a Psychology of Being,* Chap. 3, "Deficiency Motivation and Growth Motivation."

7. Loren Eiseley, *The Immense Journey* (New York: Vintage Books, Random House, 1957), pp. 125-26.

8. Charles Reich, *The Greening of America* (New York: Random House, 1970), p. 4.

CHAPTER 2

Creating a Growth Environment—
The Group's Formation and Flow

In a season of active growth, the grass in a well-maintained lawn, 50 by 50 feet, liberates enough oxygen to meet the needs of a family of four day after day.

"LAWNCARE"[1]

A GROWTH GROUP is an experience in good human ecology. Like the lawn described above, it produces the "oxygen" of communication and caring—as vital to your personality as physical oxygen is to your body. An effective group provides the fresh air of honesty and acceptance to awaken spirits dulled by the smog of manipulative relationships and the loneliness of a bureaucratic society. As renewal occurs, members become oxygen givers in their relationships. The individual attends a group session to find fulfillment for himself; finding this involves him in the growth of others. Thus, in self-renewal, he becomes a renewal agent for others. This is the refreshing serendipity of growth groups!

The structures, process, and leadership style which promote this vitalizing of people will be the subjects of Chapter 2 and 3. Although these matters may seem to be exclusive concerns of group leaders, knowledge of the formation and operation of groups can also be useful to group *members*. For one thing, knowledge on this level helps establish growth-stimulating group relationships. If growth is to occur, the split between the "expert" leader and the passive follower must go—a split which has proved to be a key reason why people do *not* grow significantly in some groups. Obviously, the designated leader should have special competence and skills. One of his functions is to help members learn the skills required to become mutual growth facilitators. To produce a *growth* group, members must "own" the group by sharing in decisions about its operation and goals. Each member acquires a piece of the leadership responsibility.

The realization that there is no hocus-pocus in growth-group leadership should inspire confidence on the part of a would-be leader to acquire leadership training and then start a group. If you "turn on" to life through people, in a group situation, you may decide to join the chain-reaction movement of creating growth opportunities for others. An understanding of the inner workings of growth groups will strengthen your basis for doing this. Let's look at some key factors in the creation of a growth environment.

LENGTH AND FREQUENCY

One strength of the growth-group approach is its adaptability to a variety of formats. The challenge is to be aware of the needs of your group and to develop formats which meet those needs best. Innovate and experiment until you discover what's best for your unique situation. To suggest the range of possibilities, here are some growth-group formats which have been used effectively:

Weekly meeting of one and a half to two hours—the "standard" approach drawn from the group psychotherapy model.

A three- to six-hour meeting every other week—e.g., Sunday afternoon, or a long evening beginning perhaps with a snack meal.

An all day meeting—8:30 A.M. to 6:00 or 8:30 P.M.—once a month. (Groups with the above formats vary in length from three to twelve months and more.)

An intensive weekend—Friday evening through Sunday after lunch— in a renewal retreat, human relations plunge, growth happening, etc.

A nonstop, twenty-four-hour marathon. Those who need to sleep do so in the room where growth work is continuing. To avoid inter- rupting the flow, meals are brought in.

(As a general rule, concentrated growth meetings should be followed by a series of at least three or four weekly sessions to help partici- pants continue growth work and apply their learnings to their everyday living.)

An intensive three- to ten-day growth seminar or workshop, combining small growth groups and larger groups for growth-stimulation through awareness exercises, mini-lectures, role-playing, creative films, etc.

A regular weekly session of one and one-half to two and one-half hours with a mini-marathon (six to twelve hours) once every month or two. The extended sessions intensify sharing, deepen group trust, and help those who find it difficult to risk being open.

Many other formats have been effective. What *is* important, in any format, is that it provide sufficient *frequency, intensity,* and *continuity* of experience together so that the psychological process of *becoming* a group will operate. If sessions are too infrequent, time is wasted at each session getting reconnected and moving to significant communication. Groups with sessions of one and a half to two hours should meet at least every other week; weekly sessions are better, particularly during the first launching-into- group-orbit phase. Established groups which know how to move to a growth-work level rapidly can use one-hour weekly sessions productively. Sessions of one and a half hours or longer, allow- ing a significant period of time after the reconnecting, warm-up period, are preferable.

Extended sessions such as marathons (mini- and maxi-) and retreats have real value. In training lay caring teams, using monthly, three-hour sessions, we have found that an initial, all-day Saturday session helps trainees and trainers achieve a growth-group orbit much more rapidly than three-hour monthly training events by themselves. An extended session, particularly in a sequestered spot isolated from usual surroundings, has a pressure-cooker effect, accelerating the group process. Trust and group rapport build rapidly; even shy persons are often surprised and delighted with their openness. Extended sessions can give a dragging group a growth-boost. Groups can be large and still produce growth, if they have extended sessions periodically.

The most productive groups, in my experience, have decided upon a specific termination date. (Groups reaching the date can negotiate to set another target date, if this is possible and desirable.) Length should be decided in light of a particular group's growth goals. Six to eight sessions are usually minimal for achieving even modest feeling-level goals. Schools and churches which plan on a September to June basis often use that period for growth groups. One church which has several growth groups divides this period into three ten-week sessions, with a break of three weeks between them. Some schedule-burdened people will commit themselves to six to eight sessions but won't join long-term or open-ended groups.

A closing date motivates earlier and more persistent growth work. A "finis" in the future promotes growth in coping with feelings about termination and loss. Most important, a time limit poses the crucial question for experiencing the people dynamic in our kind of society: "Can I learn to relate quickly and in mutually-satisfying depth with these fellow human beings?" We must use even our brief encounters as genuine meetings. If we wait for "enough time" or "just-right" circumstances for significant relating, we may never find them.

Ongoing, open-ended groups, with good leadership, often develop intense mutual support. One clergyman who, over a two-year period, has worked with several couples groups in his church, reports that after a year or so they become "almost like a family." Such growth-support groups are invaluable to participants, but they require a major investment of the leader's time, often more than can be offered to one group, unless competent lay leaders can be developed.

What about *open* versus *closed* group membership? Ongoing groups eventually need to replace graduates and dropouts. Yet, each newcomer presents a problem as well as a growth opportunity—e.g., dealing with the anxiety/resentment aroused by his "invading" a comfortable social organism; encountering a new personality; experiencing the process of integrating him into the group identity. Each time a newcomer is added (or an old member lost), the group becomes a different group and must work through to a new sense of identity. If this happens too often, the group's trust and communication never reaches a high growth level. It is best in short-term groups with personal growth goals *not* to add members after the second session. When members (or leaders) are added or subtracted, in any group, it's essential for everyone's feelings to be discussed openly so that group identity can be rebuilt.

SMALL ENOUGH TO SHARE AND CARE

The size of a group helps determine whether it becomes a growth environment. One member declared: "Our group is like an oasis in my personal desert." This state can be achieved only through the trust-building communication possible in a relatively small group.

You'll get and give the most when you communicate frequently and directly with other group members. In groups larger than ten or twelve, the amount of time each member has to communicate with others and work on his own personal growth goals is too limited. You'll feel frustrated. Members of a group of six have fifteen relationships with which they must deal to interact as a group. A group of eight persons has 28 potential relationships; a group of 10 has 45; a group of 15 has 105; and a group of 20 has the staggering possibility of 190 relationships![2]

This explains why seven to twelve members, plus leader or co-leaders, is an optimal number for a growth group. There is a greater chance of achieving a sense of caring and community— i.e., becoming a true group—if the number of relational bridges which must be built is relatively small. Groups of less than five, however, provide too few opportunities for the growth-stimulus of encountering a variety of personalities, life experiences, values, and perspectives. And the absence of one or two members depletes the interaction severely.

Optimal size is influenced by other considerations. If you're beginning as a growth facilitator, start with a group of six or seven relatively healthy people. In a larger group, so much will happen all at once that you and the group may become confused. The more skills you acquire, the larger the group you'll be able to lead toward growth. The higher the maturity level of a prospective group, the larger it can be (usually not over fourteen). A reliable index of maturity is the degree of genuine self-esteem the individual possesses (as contrasted with a kind of "cover-up" self-sufficiency which hides low self-esteem). Genuine self-esteem is the "I'm o.k., you're o.k.,"[3] feeling. Groups are self-esteem replenishing stations but they're most effective with those who have a foundation of self-worth to build on. Groups with several people suffering from distressingly low self-esteem should be kept small—or such persons should be helped to find personal therapy.

A skilled co-leader or *natural growth catalyst* among the members permits a group to be larger and still produce growth. Persons who are self-affirming automatically affirm others. Whether they became so via previous therapeutic or growth experiences or as a result of having "chosen their parents well," they invariably help a group develop a growth climate. Their spontaneous self-honesty and nondefensiveness provide a catalyst for others. They are very different from persons who appear to have "arrived" but are actually hurting deeply behind their facade; such persons tend to inhibit, not stimulate, group growth.[4] The real catalyst is willing to share where he is in the here-and-now, where he is hurting, hoping, finding fragments of meaning, and connecting with others.

In describing natural catalysts, I have also been discussing the way in which you as group member or leader can help develop a growth-group climate. The implicit invitation open to each participant is to become a growth facilitator. The reciprocal truths are these—you help others grow by struggling openly to grow yourself, *and* you help yourself grow by sharing in growth interactions with others. This is the growth-nurturing *complementarity* of the people dynamic.

Goals of a particular group influence decisions on optimal size. A group with narrowly focused goals can be larger and still achieve the growth desired. The *level* of understanding desired also influences decisions on size and format. One group, for example, wanted "to understand the psychological needs of our pre-teens more fully." If growth in head-level understanding is the objective, a group can be large. What this group wanted was both head- and heart-level understanding of their preadolescents. The school psychologist (a resource person in their planning sessions) suggested that achieving this goal would require opportunities to discuss their own feelings, anxieties, and expectations regarding their pre-teens. Consequently, the total group—some forty parents—divided into five sharing groups for part of each of six evening sessions, with a teacher or school counselor and parent co-leaders in each small group. At each meeting, head-level ideas and feeling-provoking questions were discussed by the psychologist in an initial mini-lecture to the large group. Heart-level insight came through the small growth-discussion groups and through husband-wife communication between meetings.

The model used in this series lends itself to many conferences and ongoing growth experiences involving larger numbers. I have participated in workshops and retreats with fifty or more persons and witnessed a growth atmosphere develop in the group as a whole. This was achieved through both small growth-group sessions and through shared experiences in the total group—awareness exercises, role-playing, facing negative feelings about aspects of the workshop, group planning sessions, spontaneous happenings, parties and celebrations. The effectiveness of the *therapeutic community* approach[5] in institutions (often in wards and living units of fifty or more) and the success of *multiple-family therapy*, in which several families totaling up to forty persons meet to work collaboratively on family problems,[6] show that people can experience personal healing and growth in larger groups. Obviously, growth methods can be applied with significant results in larger groups—e.g., in churches, schools, and other institutions.

A MEETING PLACE FOR GROWTH

As to meeting places, the only requirements are *privacy* to avoid interruptions and *comfort* so that creature concerns will not interfere with growth work. Too much comfort—large, soft, overstuffed chairs, for instance—can make interaction difficult. A rug helps by encouraging floor-sitting which somehow reduces stuffy, surface relating. Sequestered meeting places for extended sessions tend to create a relaxed, open atmosphere; they also encourage participants to stay aboard and not find excuses to leave early. A group should meet where those who wish to can drink coffee and smoke. Although members' living rooms sound ideal, I can recall times when phone calls, doorbells, children, and "hostess" behavior almost wiped out growth opportunities. Each time a group changes meeting places, it must deal (overtly or covertly) with feelings about being a group in a different setting. Occasionally this can be productive of self-awareness—e.g., the dramatic differences noted in the interaction of one group in a church classroom and in a cabin at the beach!

RECRUITING A GROWTH GROUP

How you assemble a growth group depends on the setting. A general invitation in your organization's newsletter, giving a clear, attractive picture of the nature of the proposed group, may produce some "takers." Usually such an impersonal invitation must be followed by phone calls to likely prospects. If you're in an organization with ongoing educational, task, or fellowship groups, an efficient start might be to see whether persons in one or several of those groups would be interested in a special six- to eight-week growth experience. Study groups may be receptive to the idea of introducing a special "relationship training" dimension into their ongoing program. Take advantage of natural constellations of people by offering groups with growth goals relevant to needs.

If you're on an agency staff, you doubtless know at least a half dozen prospective clients— e.g., recent graduates of therapy—who would profit from a continued growth-support group. If you're a clergyman, you undoubtedly know six to eight persons (whom you've counseled and others) who would be receptive to such an invitation. A productive group in one church was formed by inviting all couples married within the last five years to join a six-week Marriage Enrichment group. Five couples accepted and formed a group.

Another church[7] started growth groups after the minister and his wife had had satisfying group experiences at a renewal center.

Reporting that they "wanted this experience" for their church, they announced the formation of an eight-session Couples' Growth group in the newsletter. Seven couples responded. This proved to be productive and several participants went on to personal growth workshops outside the church. Eventually some of these persons became leaders of groups for college youth. After participants in an initial group have a fulfilling experience, an organization's "grapevine" usually carries the good news—that something need-satisfying is happening—and others inquire about joining a group.

The invitation, announced goals, and name of your group should fit the felt needs of your people. Any invitation, written or oral, should state clearly that personal growth (enrichment, development, fulfillment, strengthening) is a primary purpose. The best names for adult groups in most settings are low-key and non-exotic. Emphasize the positive, growth-orientation by using terms such as: "Enrichment Group," "Relationship Training Fellowship," "Growth Workshop," "Personal Effectiveness Group," "Human Potentials Group," "Renewal Group," "I.P.R. (Inter-Personal Relations) Group," "Search and Discovery Group," "Marriage Enrichment Group," "Self-Discovery Group," "Learning for Living Group," etc. Where the extremists, who constitute a small but noisy segment of the group scene, make people hyperanxious regarding all groups, it's best to use very low-threat labels such as "Sharing Group," "Support Group," "Personal Study Group," "Training for Caring Group," "Share and Care Group." Relating the groups to accepted institutional activities—"Bible Growth Group" in a church or "Teacher Effectiveness Training" in an educational setting, for example—helps to keep them both relevant and accepted. "Sensitivity training" and even "encounter group" are loaded terms for many who would respond to a nonthreatening group name geared to their needs and acceptable within their organizations. Offer a choice of groups with different names and approaches, to meet the varying needs of people you wish to reach.

Two forms of resistance often deter group prospects. One is the erroneous belief that a growth group, whatever its name, is for "people with big problems." A minister who has been successful in developing a network of groups, suggests that one way of handling this objection is to recruit solid leader-types within the institution for the first group. When word gets around that *these people* are in a growth group, the "disturbed-persons" image will be dealt a decisive blow. The other form of resistance is the expressed fear that "If I come, I'll be pressured to drag all the old skeletons out of the closet." This is met in recruiting marriage groups. Emphasizing the here-and-now *growth* focus, and the nonarchaeological (no digging up old bones) approach of the group, reduces this fear.

SELECTION OF MEMBERS

Experience has shown that some people profit more from growth groups than others and some probably shouldn't join at all. Careful screening of potential members is not always feasible, but the leader should try to identify those who are likely not to profit. This can be done before the first session by individual meetings with persons the leader does not know. Unsuitable persons may be referred to other types of groups more likely to meet their needs: fellowship groups for those who mainly desire support and sociability; ordinary classes for those who seek intellectual growth; and counseling or therapy groups for those with high anxiety, precarious self-esteem, or disintegrated relationships. People with deeply disturbed relationships will constantly pull interaction toward themselves, ignoring the growth needs of more functional members. For example, a couple with a crumbling marriage inadvertently joined a "Making the Most of Marriage" group. The intensity of their problems prevented the group from engaging in enlivening the functional marriages of the other four couples. Realizing their needs were not being met, the couple left the growth group after a few weeks to find the marital therapy they needed.

Almost anyone can benefit from a growth group if he has reasonably functional relationships, some appreciable degree of self-esteem, and a desire to improve his relationships, his inner vitality, or the use of his talents. Those who ordinarily cope adequately with life's demands, but are temporarily staggering from a heavy blow, can use a growth group to extract latent growth possibilities from the crisis.

A young couple, married for two years and enjoying many satisfactions in their relationship, wanted a stronger bond and better communication. So they joined a couples growth group.

A teen-age girl, coping well with her school- and peer-relationships, felt confused by the value choices facing her. She accepted the suggestion of a counselor and joined a teen "Search for Meaning" group led by her pastor.

A recently retired man, searching for new fulfillment to replace his successful job experience, joined a sharing group called "Using Your Retirement Constructively," sponsored by a center for older adults.

These are but a few examples of people who made good use of growth experiences.

THE INITIAL MEETING

The goals of the first session include getting acquainted, starting to share on a significant level, and gaining consensus concerning purposes of the group and what each person expects to receive and give in the process (called the group "contract" or "covenant"). Here is the way I often begin. After asking the group to move into a smaller circle (they're often spacially as well as emotionally separated at the start), I introduce myself and tell a bit about the general objectives of such a group; then I invite group members to introduce themselves and say why they came and what they hope to achieve in the group. It is important —during the first session—to give each person an opportunity to describe his growth goals.

There is a variety of ways to get connected as a group—joining hands in the circle with eyes closed for a moment and then discussing what each person experienced; milling around, taking a brief time to hold the hands and look into the eyes of each member, repeating his name; talking in pairs for a few minutes about topics such as "What I hope for and fear in this group," "What's most important to me right now," "What I hope to become in the next year," after which each person introduces his partner to the group, sharing what he has learned. Discussion of any of these queries usually moves a group into significant sharing.

Here is another way to start. After brief self-introductions, the leader may say:

"Well, here we are. We have seven sessions to work together on our personal goals. Each of us has unused strengths and assets, and some ideas about using these more fully. As I see it, the main purpose of the group is to support each person in moving toward his own goals. I'm looking forward to this because I know that groups like this can be helpful to both leader and members. But right now, I'm also feeling a little uptight—anxious, I guess. I'm wondering how you're feeling."

It is important that the leader be candid about his feelings at that moment. By so doing, he demonstrates the behavior that will help the group move from superficial to significant communication. Anxiety in the beginning group is often "so thick you can cut it." Open sharing about this feeling tends to reduce it to productive levels. The leader should encourage the expression of doubts, reservations, resistance, fears, and negative feelings about previous group experiences. Positive feelings and hopes will also emerge. It is crucial to discover and encourage full expression of resentment by those who have been nagged or dragged to come—often by well-meaning spouses. Drawing out (and respecting) these feelings, and the person's own growth goals, offers the only real hope of helping such a person to join the group for his own reasons.

The group covenant begins to take form as leader and members express their hopes and expectations for the group. Differences in individual goals need not hinder a group's effectiveness, providing all members are interested in some form of personal growth. Discussion and agreement on group guidelines, sometime during the first session, is an essential part of the covenant. I often suggest some or all of these to a group (depending on the group and the circumstances):

"Let me suggest some guidelines which can help make groups like this useful to their members. One is that *everyone's views and feelings are valued*. The group will be helpful to the extent that we speak openly and listen to each other. It helps keep things on a personal level if we try to speak in the first person singular—'I feel . . .' or 'I experience this in this way . . .'—rather than using the third person or general statements like, 'Most people feel . . .'" (Group discussion)

"Another guideline that seems to help groups is that *our main attention be on current happenings*—relationships and problems we face and also what goes on among us in the group.* Thus we avoid spending time in the past rather than where the action is—in the now. A related guideline is that if significant things happen between any of us outside the group, we share them with the group; otherwise some good growth opportunities for the whole group will be missed. Do these guidelines sound useful?" (Discussion)

"Many groups agree among themselves that *what others say in the*

---

* If you wish to limit the depth of interaction, focus only on personal problems from outside the group, not on relationships within it.

group will be treated as confidential; this is to free everyone to discuss whatever is on his mind. Do you feel that this would be useful?" (Discussion)

"This can be a richer experience if new insights and ways of relating which develop here are *used between sessions.* Applying our findings in our everyday lives lets us discover whether we have really learned them. Is this a reasonable expectation?" (Discussion)

"Groups like this become effective if members agree to *give them priority* and to attend sessions unless prevented by illness or serious problems from doing so." (Discussion)

"Some people get discouraged after a few sessions and drop out. If you should feel this way, I'd like to suggest that you *attend at least the first four or five sessions* before you make a decision.* It takes at least that long to discover whether this kind of group will be helpful to you. If you then decide that the group is not your cup of tea, that is o.k. Just come to the group and discuss it, so that others can complete unfinished growth business with you. How do you feel about these guidelines?" (Discussion and decisions about which guidelines to use in the group.)

Some facilitators prefer to have no group guidelines or ground rules except perhaps the one about sharing fully and openly. Avoid presenting guidelines so that they sound like a federal case. They can be useful in helping a group move toward deeper trust and communication; they can reduce frustrations and hazards—but, unless the group senses their usefulness and owns them, they become symbols of leader-dominance. Members should be free to modify or reject any suggested guidelines and offer others. The important thing is that the group discuss its way through to a *consensus as a part of a common commitment to shared growth work.*

---

* This guideline is relevant only if members haven't committed themselves to a certain number of sessions in agreeing to join the group.

STAGES IN THE LIFE OF A GROUP

Every group, like every individual, has a unique life history and identity. There are, however, some typical stages growth groups tend to go through in developing as environments of renewal.

Stage 1: *Initial anxiety, testing, and attempts at connecting.* In the early meetings there is considerable defensiveness (because of anxiety), testing of each other and the leader, and attempts to relate in some meaningful way. To reduce their anxieties about new relationships, some members usually push the leader to take over and "run" the group. If the facilitator falls into this trap, the group will stay leader-dependent and never become a growth group. The leader can introduce enough structure—e.g., content material, a brief lecturette, or awareness exercise—to reduce anxiety and stimulate interaction, providing he uses it in a group-centered manner. The discussion about what each person wants and expects from the group and the decisions about guidelines move the group toward a sense of cohesion and common purpose. In the early sessions members usually focus on problems rather than potentials. The leader, in each stage, affirms unused strengths and resources in individuals and in the group as a whole. However there can be little depth-sharing and mutual growth-stimulation until stronger group rapport develops.

Stage 2: *The honeymoon.* The dominant feelings at this stage are euphoria and enjoyment of group camaraderie. One elated group member exclaimed, "It's great to have a place where you can let your hair down, be honest about your hangups, and know others are in the same boat!" Actually, the relatedness experienced at the start is only a foretaste of the caring of a mature growth group. Most of the feelings expressed during the honeymoon stage are warm and positive. Members luxuriate in the warming awareness that their painful loneliness is being invaded by people.

Stage 3: *Frustration and questioning.* In this stage there may be a spirit of group depression, flatness, and disillusion. This frustration phase is more or less intense depending on the group. These feelings stem from reluctance to risk going deeper, resistance to owning the group, and anxiety about trusting the group with one's real pain. What seemed easy during the honeymoon, now looks flat, difficult, even impossible. Anger surfaces toward the leader who "doesn't lead"—at least not in the way we want when we're anxious. The leader may discourage dropouts by mentioning that some may feel like bailing out. His most important function is to help the group reflect critically on its own mood and interaction, to express their negative feelings openly, and to re-evaluate the goals of the experience with a no-holds-barred honesty. The struggle, conflict, and questioning are the narrow gate through which groups must go to achieve genuine intimacy and become an environment for growth. The leader shouldn't try to rescue the group (even though he's tempted) or attempt to cheer them up; his efforts should be directed toward helping them face rather than run from group conflict and frustration. In struggling together they will discover how difficult it is to connect in depth with other human beings, yet they will take giant steps toward achieving such relationships, individually and as a group. This stage is a clear illustration of the principle that growth involves struggle and pain. Old patterns of defensiveness and distancing must die before new closeness can be born.

Stage 4: *Risking and trusting.* Gradually, some members begin to risk openness by sharing their disappointments, their pain, their dim hopes for change. Their openness is a catalyst encouraging others to drop their facades. Communication moves to a new level; both caring and confrontation are given and received. Members discover that they *can* trust the group and risk being open; when they do, they experience the acceptance of the group supporting and warming them. Group ownership is firming up.

The group will attempt to complete itself by drawing silent members in: e.g., "Your silence makes me feel that I don't really know you. Somehow I feel cheated." Gradually, most, if not all, members experience sufficient trust to take the leap of honest sharing, discovering therein the key to deeper relationships. Members and leader can point to the growth-blocking attitudes and behavior which prevent the use of potential. The group has now reached the level when collaborative "growth work" can be undertaken wholeheartedly with group support.

Stage 5: *Effective growth work.* Changes in individuals and in relationships begin to occur during stage 4; they flourish in stage 5. Members work to help one another move toward growth goals. Progress and breakthroughs are rewarded by affirming group responses. Spontaneous cheers and handclapping are not unusual. These group affirmations of growth help to stabilize new self-images and behavior. Changes in self-esteem are reflected in statements such as: "You see me as worthwhile and you know more about my messy side than anyone . . . It's easier to like myself." Behavior and relationship growth is also evident. In marriage groups, couples begin to report that they've been able to get through their inner walls between sessions, interrupt self-defeating behavior, and stay friends longer. Group members who didn't set realistic goals initially are now confronted firmly by a group that cares enough not to look the other way while they live at a fraction of their potential. Leadership-facilitator functions are now shared widely within the group. *Concern* for others' growth is now implemented by *skills* learned mainly from the leader's ways of relating. Mutual growth-work is radically different from the superficial problem-solving of early sessions, described by a group member as "everyone playing Mr. Fix-It to keep the group away from him."

Because group ownership is well established, the leader can now function increasingly as a group member. He can deal with his own loneliness and growth needs if he chooses. I'm assuming that he has related as a human being—with the full range of feelings—from the beginning; now he and the group will be helped if he participates fully in mutual growth work.

At any stage, but particularly now, the group and/or the leader may suggest renegotiating the original covenant; in the birth of awareness and new behavior, new growth needs and goals have become evident. Ups and downs will continue to occur in the group's climate and interaction. In fact, a plateau is often reached following an emotionally intense session.

Stage 6: *Closing.* Terminating a group should be a gradual, growth-productive process. In each of several sessions before the end, the group should be reminded of how much time is left and asked how they feel about this. Raising this issue usually triggers growth-work that members have been resisting. A group which has achieved a sense of caring and community approaches termination with grief feelings. Coping with these in the group produces growth in the ability to live constructively with the series of losses which is an inescapable part of life.

In a sense, the closing of each meeting is a loss experience if significant relating has occurred. There are four things I do, at least in a brief way, at the end of nearly every session, and in a more systematic manner as a group's termination nears: (1) Attempt to deal with unfinished feelings and relating. Simply asking, "Does anyone feel that something is unfinished?" usually suffices. Even if the issues or relationship problems can't be resolved, it helps for the group to recognize the unfinished concerns as important. (2) Ask what continuing growth goals and plans there are. This future-orientation encourages continuing growth work between sessions and after a group's conclusion. Stating goals in the group firms them up and strengthens commitment. (3) Ask the group to evaluate the session (or the entire group experience). This surfaces hidden hurts and angers so that they can be resolved or at least verbalized. Otherwise, they'll fester between or after the group meetings. Regular end-of-session evaluations give the leader a reading on group progress and needed changes. Evaluations at termination provide valuable data for planning other groups. (4) Leave-taking. Symbolizing and celebrating what has been experienced together give a group a sense of completion. Standing in an "affirmation circle" while people express their feelings about the group and about parting is one among many ways to do this. The best leave-takings are impromptu expressions by the group—a spontaneous song, a dance, a prayer, or some other celebration of growth. In one closing circle, a man stated his experience in words which articulate what growth groups have meant to many of us: "All my adult life I've believed with my head that 'no man is an island.' Now, I know it with my heart and *that makes all the difference!*"

REFERENCES

1. "Lawncare," (Cover), Fall 1970, California edition. (Scotts Products.)
2. Robert Hare, *Handbook of Small Group Research* (New York: Free Press, 1970), pp. 228 ff. To understand this, draw lines between dots (in a circle) representing your group's members.
3. Thomas Harris, *I'm O.K.; You're O.K.* (New York: Harper & Row, 1969).
4. One common expression of the fear of getting involved with one's own hurt is to play "leader"; this is an attempt to keep others controlled and at a safe distance by being "helpful." Such a person is often "an old hand at groups," but his behavior keeps the group from becoming a growth experience for him.
5. Maxwell Jones, *Beyond the Therapeutic Community* (New Haven: Yale University Press, 1968).
6. Psychiatrist Norman Paul of Boston has pioneered this approach.
7. The First United Methodist Church, Tucson, Ariz.; DeWane Zimmerman, Minister.

CHAPTER 3

Leadership and Tools
for Growth Groups

My hope is gradually to become as much a participant in the group as a facilitator. . . . If you watch a group member who is honestly being himself, you will see that at times he expresses feelings, attitudes, and thoughts primarily directed toward facilitating the growth of another member. At other times, with equal genuineness, he will express feelings of concerns which have as their obvious goal the opening of himself to the risk of more growth. This describes me, too. . . .

CARL ROGERS[1]

THE KEY to any group's ability to release the people dynamic is the nature and quality of its leadership. The process described in Chapter 2 usually will evolve if the leader possesses growth-facilitating skills and is himself a growing person. The same qualities and skills which are essential to the creation of growth groups tend to release human potential in task groups, study groups, supportive-inspiration groups, and others.

The leader-facilitator brings his know-how and personhood to the group as resources for doing three things: (1) facilitating the growth of individual members; (2) developing a group climate and style of relating which release individual members and the group as a growth-stimulating organism; (3) continuing his own growth. Carl Jung once suggested that the test of an effective psychotherapeutic relationship is whether or not it produces change in both the therapist and the patient. This criterion also applies to growth experiences. If the leader risks and grows, most group members will also.

GROWTH-LEADERSHIP FUNCTIONS

What does the leader do to facilitate growth in a group?

1. *He assembles and launches the group* (as described in the last chapter).

2. *By example, he teaches growth-awakening relating.* A growth-facilitating style is caught by members as much as taught. The leader tries to be as self-revealing, caring, and trustful of the group as he would like them to become. A recent graduate offered this sound advice on enhancing my effectiveness in teaching: "Howard, let it all hang out!" Translated, this means let people know you, risk sharing yourself, including your struggles and vulnerability and love. A leader helps the group move from superficial socializing to need-satisfying relating by sharing his own feelings and responding to the feelings of others. He listens, not as an expert to a needy client, but as one hurting, hoping human being to another. He knows that every individual cries out for affirmation as a unique person. He encourages listening that affirms—listening to a person's words and to feelings that are too painful or precious to trust to words—by listening and responding on this level himself. ("Let's see if I hear you, Joe, in this thing with your son . . ."). At first members barely listen to themselves or each other; with help, they tune in on the wavelength of feelings. They do what Paul Tillich called "loving listening."

3. *The leader facilitates development of group identity* through significant relating and sharing. He does this by fostering group-centered interaction. By *linking* behavior he encourages members

to look to each other for understanding and help. In an early-stage group where most communicating is toward him, he may observe: "Sally, that sounds to me like what Bill was saying earlier. Do you two see any connection?" Or: "Jerry, you've been through a situation similar to Mac's. What would you say about it?" When messages ricochet off him to others, the leader may invite the senders to speak directly to the intended receivers.

The facilitator fosters group-centeredness by not playing "expert answer-man" or the usual teacher or leader roles. Here's a segment from a marriage enrichment group (session one):

Group member: (to leader) "It might help us get started if you would tell us what sort of things we should discuss in a group like this."
Leader: "I'll be glad to share my ideas, but I'm sure some of you have ideas about how you'd like to see us use the group. What do you think?"

By avoiding the authority-centered role, the leader puts the responsibility where it belongs—on the group—thus helping them activate and use their own resources. In psychiatrist Eric Berne's terms the leader mobilizes the members' Adult sides by refusing to play Parent/Child (leader/follower) games.[2] This is more than a technique for developing group-centeredness. It's an expression of the leader's trust in the releasable inner resources of each individual, trust in the group as a potentially helpful organism, and trust in the process by which the people dynamic in individuals and groups is released. Implementing this trust is a crucial function of a growth facilitator.

4. *The leader maintains awareness of both the individual and the group organism.* He tries to stay tuned to the changing moods, themes, waves, interaction patterns and levels of both. As individuals share in significant ways, their worlds of experience and meaning begin to overlap, producing a new reality—the group. Like any other organism, the group is more than the sum of its

parts. A unique life and "personality" of its own develop. This organism becomes a growth-stimulating environment.

The leader seeks (never succeeding fully) to maintain whole-group awareness and to foster this in members so that they can improve their group's interaction.

Leader: (to group as a whole) "How would you describe our relating during the last half hour or so?"
Curt: "We're on a head-trip, playing it safe!" (Agreement in group.)
Leader: "Any feelings about this?"
Curt: "I'm damn mad at the group and myself. Let's stop avoiding each other!"

Consider this facilitator's comment to a group that had gone flat: "I'm at a loss to know what's going on right now. I get a blaah feeling. How do the rest of you see it?" This honest leveling did several things. It mobilized group efforts at self-awareness and self-understanding; it dispelled the flatness by precipitating here-and-now involvement; and it freed the leader from any pretense of always being "on top of it," tuned in, fully aware.

5. *The leader focuses on releasing the unused potentialities of individuals and the group, thus encouraging group members to do the same.* Small groups tend to do postmortems of old failures, archaeologizing (digging in the past for explanations of present behavior), and pathologizing (focusing more on problems than potentials). While dealing with those lively spooks from the past* which influence present behavior profoundly, the facilitator puts at least equal emphasis on the present and the future: What do you want and hope for? What must you do now to move toward it? When the past comes up, it is related to the present and future: "How does that relate to your current situation and goals?"

Leader: (At a family growth retreat) "If your family is anything like

* For example, strong inner dependency ties with parents must be severed before a person is free to grow as an adult in his own unique direction.

ours, we could spend all weekend analyzing past mistakes and present problems. But how about a different approach—some discussion of the things we like about our families and some planning in each family of what we want to build on these strengths in the next year?"

This approach communicates hope and affirmation: you *have* the power to move toward change in your family.

We tend to hide our light from ourselves as well as others. A caring group can help you discover the latent person within you with all his unused possibilities.

Leader: "Jim, you seem to be down on yourself. Would you be interested in what group members see as your assets and strengths?"

Along with emphasizing the choosing of realistic growth goals, a leader encourages planning and taking steps toward achieving them. In-group practice of new communication and relationship skills permits mutual coaching and nurturing of growth.

6. *The leader encourages the group to employ the growth formula—caring plus confrontation produces growth.* A confrontation without caring triggers only defensiveness. It is caring —so much that one refuses to ignore self-defeating behavior—that elicits self-awareness. The New Testament describes such loving confrontation as "speaking the truth in love" (Eph. 4:15).

7. *The leader offers tools for enhancing communication and practicing deeper relating.* These include awareness exercises, expressive uses of art, role playing, dispensing useful information, among others. When used appropriately, these tools can increase interaction, move a blocked group off dead center, and give access to hidden feelings.

8. *The leader helps individuals who need further support or involvement.* Occasionally, in small groups, someone's circuits are overloaded by anxiety or too much confrontation (in relation to

the degree of trust present). Rigidity, withdrawal, or consistent defensiveness may indicate this. In well-functioning groups, members usually sense what is happening and respond supportively. In new groups, however, or with persons who are easily rejected or emotionally raw from crisis, temporary leader-support may be necessary. An empathetic "You've been through a rough experience!" or an affirming "It takes guts to survive in that kind of situation" will usually suffice. (I am assuming that the leader will say only what he means sincerely.) Information-level (as contrasted with feeling-level) responses or questions can help by providing breathing-space and some distance from powerful feelings. A supportive leader-response can often be followed productively by a question aimed at activating the person's strong side—e.g., *Leader*: "How would you describe the way you were feeling a few minutes ago?" In Berne's terms, support usually quiets the frightened Child side so that the inner Adult side can gain control and begin coping constructively.

If a person seems disturbed at the end of a session, the leader should give support by talking with him briefly. If this doesn't suffice, the leader may suggest an individual session. Persons seen individually should be encouraged to describe to the next group meeting what transpired.

Growth-enabling leadership is best described as "maieutic" leadership, from the Greek *maieuomu* (to serve as midwife). Its function is to assist the natural process by which human beings experience the birth of self-other awareness and grow in their ability to cope constructively with their life situation.

THE GROUP MEMBER AS LEADER

During the early meetings of a group, the designated leader fulfills most of the leadership functions. But, as has been indicated, he starts sharing the leadership almost from the beginning by drawing the group into decision-making about goals and by encouraging them to respond to each other in growth-facilitative ways. When groups reach the growth-work stage, members participate in all major leader-facilitator functions. One can recognize a mature growth group by its lack of leader dependence, its high level of trust and mutual confrontation, the ways in which growth facilitation occur throughout the group, and the ways in which the designated leader draws on group resources. As Rogers observes (in the quote opening this chapter), functions aimed at facilitating one's own growth and those aimed at facilitating growth in others are shared by members and designated leaders.

Are growth groups without a designated leader feasible? In any group a competent leader increases the likelihood of growth and reduces the risk of the group's withering from frustration or causing emotional wounds. However, many groups which have reached a "growth work" level with a leader can then function productively without him because members have mastered leadership skills. Some beginning groups without a designated leader become productive because one or more members possess facilitative skills acquired in previous growth experiences. In leaderless groups without such persons, four factors can contribute to a growth-productive outcome: relatively "healthy" members, modest growth goals, considerable structure, and avoidance of major focusing on intragroup relationships. The less structure and the more ambitious goals a group has, the more essential a skilled leader becomes. Leaderlessness tends to produce "jockeying for position" among natural leaders; this can be reduced by a group decision regarding a convener or rotating chairman. Leaderlessness often releases latent resources within a group and there is some highly suggestive evidence concerning the values of leaderless groups.[3] Until more substantial research findings are available, it would seem safer and better to opt for trained leaders whenever they are available.

CO-LEADERS IN GROWTH GROUPS

Here are some of the advantages in co-leadership:

Co-leaders can give each other continuing, evaluative feedback and
compare their perceptions of group interaction.

Members have an opportunity to do growth-work vis-à-vis two different
styles of leadership and authority.

If one leader is unavailable on a given day, the continuity of the group
is not interrupted.

Male and female co-leaders provide opportunities for growth in relation to authority–figures of both sexes.

It is essential that co-facilitators keep communication open between them, particularly regarding disagreements, feeling of
rivalry, etc. Regular post-sessions for evaluating are helpful.
Ideally, co-leaders should be able to discuss their feelings, relationship, and disagreements openly in the group. This in itself
constitutes a learning experience for most group members.

COPING CONSTRUCTIVELY WITH GROUP PROBLEMS

The only way to avoid all risks and interpersonal problems is
to avoid people. The aim in growth groups is to prevent problems when possible and cope with them constructively when they
do occur. Some problems which may be encountered are:

Superficial, unproductive sessions. Most groups have arid peri-
ods. If a group seems stale, an honest evaluation by the whole
membership may help. Do members feel their needs are being
ignored, that you as leader are dominating? Are the guidelines
being followed? If a frank evaluation doesn't help, discuss the
whole situation with a more experienced group facilitator. He
may help you diagnose and treat the malady.

Silent members and monopolizers. The leader may try to
draw the silent one in or quiet the monopolizer. A better ap-

proach is to ask the group how they react to the individual involved. The question surfaces underlying feelings—e.g., anger toward the person, who can then be helped to learn from the confrontation. Silence can mean many things—fear of opening up, passive control, productive reflection. The consistently silent person should realize that others probably feel that, by his silence, he is withholding himself. The chronic monopolizer is often a manipulator who is frightened by the threat of closeness or by situations which he cannot control. He uses a verbal barrage to maintain distance and control. A combination of support and affirmation, to allay his anxieties, and firm confrontation concerning the effects of his behavior on his relationships may help. If nothing silences the verbal steamroller, it may indicate that he cannot tolerate enough closeness to benefit from a growth group.

Going deeper than is constructive. Some individuals respond in every small group as though it were depth-therapy. A leader's responses can head off self-disclosure that may be overthreatening to individuals or the group generally. Here is a rough index of threat levels of interaction:

Least threatening   Level 1—Discussing ideas, information, theories, generalizations.

↑

Level 2—Sharing personal experiences from the past.

Level 3—Sharing current problems and feelings from outside the group.

↓

Level 4—Encountering here-and-now relationships and feelings in the group.

Most threatening   Level 5—Sharing very personal problems not ordinarily discussed outside the family.

Most people can benefit significantly from sharing on levels 1, 2, and 3. Leaderless groups generally should stay on these levels; the feelings aroused by levels 4 and 5 usually require a leader's skills if they are to be used for growth. Most short-term groups with competent leaders should not go beyond level 3, mainly because there isn't enough time to work through deep feelings. Relatively inexperienced group leaders should increase their skills and confidence in levels 1 to 3 before attempting to move to 4 and 5.

If a leader senses that someone is revealing very personal problems prematurely (before group identity and trust have developed) or in an inappropriate setting (a study group, for example), he should avoid responding in ways that focus on what has been said. He should help the group share (on levels 1, 2, and 3) and not overload the feeling circuits.

The disturbed member. As suggested earlier, giving individual attention to those who seem upset is usually adequate. If it isn't, and the disturbance continues, referral to a competent psychotherapist is in order. The chances of this problem occurring are reduced drastically if the threat-level issue and proper selection of participants are taken seriously. In addition, three procedures on the leader's part reduce the risk of serious problems—working with a co-leader, having regular supervisory conferences with a more experienced growth facilitator, and continuing in one's own growth group.

There is good evidence that sensitive, supportive leadership could prevent many of the disturbances that occur in group sessions. In one study of college students suffering "an enduring, significant negative outcome" from encounter groups, it was found that groups with most of the severe problems had had aggressive, confronting, authoritarian leaders.[4]

Threatening the establishment. Opposition from persons in authority takes various forms. Some extend guilt-by-association from the extremist fringe of the group movement to all groups. Some have negative biases toward small groups because of painful experiences with rebellious, partially liberated "group-ers" in their organization. Administrators who are rigid, "organization man" types find any group which nurtures free spirits an irritant if not an outright threat to their values and life-style. Anyone who is growing and open poses a threat to those who have made a virtue of their private prisons.

How one handles opposition depends on its nature and one's power position in the organization. Good intrainstitutional diplomacy and public relations are helpful in reducing opposition to a minimum—e.g., interpreting the nature and purposes of a proposed group and obtaining official approval. Reporting on the group program to a governing board, in a way that does not violate group confidence, helps allay anxieties that could otherwise sabotage the program. If opposition is violent and not ameliorated by evidence that the group program is responsibly led and constructive, one has several alternatives. Ignore it, if your internal power position is strong; beat a strategic retreat, at least temporarily, from leading groups at all; or find a freer base of operations. It's impossible to be a liberating facilitator when you feel trapped or painfully vulnerable.

AWARENESS AND COMMUNICATION TOOLS

The group leader's knowledge of self-other awareness exercises can enhance interaction within the group. William Schutz reports:

Talking is usually good for intellectual understanding of personal experience, but it is often not as effective for helping a person to *experience*—to feel. Combining the non-verbal with the verbal seems to create a much more powerful tool for cultivating human growth.[5]

Awareness exercises can help us rediscover *immediate experiencing* and get beyond the use of words and intellectualizing to pretend, keep distance, control, hide. The exercises can help us get in touch with forgotten feelings and sensations. Most of us were programmed in childhood to ignore many rich, powerful, sensual feelings within our bodies. These disowned feelings have a destructive effect on our bodies, our spirits, and our relationships. Owned and welcomed back into our total being, they enrich and deepen us. Arthur Foster, who has made extensive use of non-verbals, declares:

These non-verbal communication methods involve the whole self— cognitive, volitional, emotive and somatic aspects. Powerfully they evoke and express depth meanings along the dimensions of: love and hate, hope and despair, freedom and bondage, the desire to know and the dread of knowing, winning and losing, strength and weakness, inclusion and exclusion, joy and flatness, individualization and communion, independence and dependence, masculinity and femininity.[6]

Awareness methods can help develop a bond of community in a remarkably short time. Some of them are excellent ways of celebrating that experience of depth communication (called communion) from which shared worlds and meanings evolve.

These methods can be misused as emotional "trips" or superficial parlor games, with no sustained value. Growth-producing use follows these ground rules: (1) Use them only as one segment of an ongoing group experience so that the learning opportunities they provide can be utilized fully. (2) Always debrief the experience by ample discussion after each exercise. In larger groups, debrief in circles of five to seven. Use only as many exercises as can be debriefed thoroughly. (3) Make it clear that each person's response is o.k. for him. There are no right and wrong ways to respond—doors to understanding and communication can be opened by positive, negative, or indifferent responses. (4) Suggest that those with physical problems (e.g., weak backs or heart conditions) not participate in vigorous exercises such as falling and catching, lifting and rocking, etc. (5) As leader, participate in the exercises, both to share the experience with the group and to avoid the impression that you are manipulating others to do things you're not willing to do yourself.

Here are some of the exercises which I have found most useful in growth groups:[7]

EXERCISES FOR INDIVIDUAL AWARENESS

These will be more meaningful if you *do* them rather than *read* about them. (The three dots indicate that the leader pauses.)

Reclaiming your inner space: "Find a comfortable position. Close your eyes so that you can concentrate on your experience. How does it feel to be inside your body? . . . What is the most tense part—put your hand on that and let go of the tension . . . Be aware of all your feelings in the present moment . . . Breathe deeply a few times . . . Now picture the space of your consciousness as a room. If you've been 'beside yourself,' move inside your inner space. Now make an effort to push back the walls and enlarge your inner room . . . How does it feel now? . . . Experience yourself in the here-and-now . . . Open your eyes and share what this experience was like."

Getting in touch with your feelings: "Close your eyes and use your ability to fantasize. Imagine a movie screen in your mind . . . On it I'd like to have you project *the happiest memory of your life*; put yourself in the action; relive the feelings that you had then; resavor that experience to the full . . . (Debrief) On the screen now project the *most unhappy experience of your life,* etc. (Debrief) Picture yourself in *your earliest memory* . . . How do you feel? Relive the experience." (Debrief)

"Close your eyes and picture yourself all alone on an island—isolated from all other human beings. You are the only survivor of a shipwreck. You have hoped for many months to be rescued. You now realize that it is unlikely that you will ever see another human being again. Experience your feelings . . . Now picture a tiny dot on the horizon . . . Gradually you can make out the shape of a small boat . . . The boat is approaching the shore; as it reaches the beach you see in the boat the person who is most important to you. You run to the boat. You embrace! Be aware of all your feelings . . ." (Debrief)

The leader or group members can vary this exercise to deal with other feelings. One of these exercises can provide enough experiencing to work on for a whole session or more.

Trappedness and freedom: "Close your eyes and using your ability to fantasize, imagine yourself in a tightly closed box. It's very small —you barely fit; it presses you on all sides. How does it feel? . . . Now, try to get out of the box . . . If you succeed, how does it feel to be free?" (Debrief)

COMMUNICATING WITH OTHERS

The following exercises are designed to provide experiences and practice in relating and communicating.

Non-verbal communication: "Get acquainted by exploring each other's hands, with eyes closed, without speaking; then open your eyes and affirm each other visually."

"With your shoes off and your eyes closed, wander around in the group, greeting each other non-verbally."

"Look into each other's eyes for one minute, without talking . . . What feeling do you sense in the other's eyes? . . . Tell each other about your experience."

"Be your feelings in the here-and-now."

"Stand quietly and feel the rhythms of your body. As you wish, begin to move to those rhythms . . . Find a partner and try to express your two rhythms together . . ."

Assertiveness, anger, competitiveness: "Pick someone about your size. Indian arm wrestle. Be aware of your feelings about winning or losing."

"Pick someone about your size. Close your eyes, grasp hands, and imagine that he's someone who annoys you. Try to push the other to the edge of the circle. Discuss your feelings."

"Beat a pillow (or a cardboard box) as hard as you can, letting out whatever sounds or words come to your lips."

"Jump up and down and shout as loudly as you can. Let it all out! . . . Let's hear it! . . . Louder!"

For persons bound up in anger—hot or cold—such exercises can give access to negative feelings and to positive ones trapped behind the dam of anger.

Trusting one another: "Stand close together in a small circle. Each person takes a turn standing in the center, eyes closed, and falling backwards, without moving his feet, to be passed around the circle by the group. Be aware of how it feels to trust the group."

Trust jogging: "Pick a partner you'd like to know better. Take turns, one with his eyes closed being led and the other doing the leading (5-15 minutes). Be sure to try to jog with your eyes closed, trusting the other . . . Discuss your feelings.

Dependence on others: "Fantasize yourself going around and standing in front of each person in your small group, saying, 'I need you.' Be aware of how it feels in each case."

"Each person take a turn lying on the floor and being lifted and rocked by the others in the group." (The group lifts each person first to waist level, rocks him gently; then lifts him over their heads, then back to waist level for brief rocking, and then gently to the floor.)

I recall one man in whom this exercise reawakened unresolved grief from the death of a loved one some fifteen years before.

Giving and receiving: "Go around the small group standing in front of each person and give him a gift—a verbal or non-verbal affirmation of him as a person."

Group unity and cohesion: "Let's join hands in the circle and feel the oneness of our group."

"Put your hands in a stack in the center. Experience your oneness. Now move your hands around in the pile and get acquainted (or reacquainted)."

"With your eyes closed, put your hand on the shoulder of the person to your right. Has your consciousness changed? Transmit caring to that person through your hand."

"Stand as close together as you feel comfortable doing. Imagine an event (or a trip, a story from the Bible, etc.) that you would like to share with our group. Plan what you and the other members of your group will do . . . Let it happen now in your fantasy; be aware of each person's part in the event . . . Now, tell one another what you experienced."

The above exercises are helpful in starting an individual session. They usually help a group begin productive communicating rapidly.

Sharing pain: "One reason we're so lonely is that we try to hide our hurt from others and pretend we are always adequate. Let me invite you to share something that really gets to you—something in your life that makes you mourn—with your small group. After each person shares, if you feel like expressing something to him, do it non-verbally, for example, by a touch or a look."

Affirming each other: The person who feels in need of group affirmation sits in the center of the circle. The group surrounds him and communicates their caring through a group embrace or the placing of hands on him.

Verbal affirmation (also known as the "strength bombardment"— psychologist Herbert Otto). Each person names what he considers to be his strengths and resources; then group members share what they consider his strengths and resources, and discuss how he might use his assets more fully.

Parting and celebration rituals: 'Stand in a circle and express (verbally or non-verbally) what catches the spirit of this session or group for you." Or "I sense that this has been a high moment for Bill and for all of us. How can we express what we feel about what has happened?"

OTHER TOOLS FOR MOVING TO THE FEELING LEVEL

Here are some other methods which help a growth group move to a level "where people live":

Going around: "Let's go around the circle and give each person a chance to say briefly how he is feeling right now" (or how he's feeling about a person or issue). This helps less aggressive members become involved.

Projecting devices: "Let me suggest that each person draw a sketch showing where he is 'feeling-wise' right now . . . (Later) On the other side of the paper draw the way you'd like to be a month from now . . . Tell the group about both."

Clay, finger paints, crayons, etc. can be used in similar ways.

"Here's a stack of magazines. On one side of this paper paste some pictures which depict your feelings about yourself and your relationships."

"Here's a sheet of paper; draw yourself as you now feel . . . Let me suggest that you give yourself a voice—write what you are saying in the picture."

Impromptu role-playing: "Would you show us what happens when you try to communicate with each other?" (in a marital growth group). "Act out a recent episode when the messages got snafued."

"Could you role-play the way you'd like to relate to your boss? This might help you get the feel of it."

A TOOL FOR UNDERSTANDING RELATIONSHIPS

Eric Berne's TA (Transactional Analysis) model of the three parts of personality—Parent/Adult/Child—provides a valuable tool for individuals, couples and groups to use in understanding and changing their relationships. Our inner Parent speaks, feels, and acts as we perceived our parents doing. This side can be constructively nurturing and limit-setting, or punishing and judgmental. Our Child side—a continuation of the way we felt as children—can be spontaneous and fun-loving, or frightened and demanding. The Adult side of our personality makes realistic decisions aimed at achieving our objectives. Growth groups seek to help people interrupt their self-damaging Child/Parent interaction and learn through practice to *keep the Adult side in charge and the nurturing, limit-setting Parent and the fun-enjoying, creative Child in healthy balance with each other.* This operational description of growth has proved a valuable tool for breaking the control of the past (Parent/Child) and learning to live in the present (Adult).

TRAINING FOR GROWTH-GROUP LEADERSHIP

Adequate training for facilitating growth groups has three essential dimensions: *growth group experience* (as a member), *conceptual understanding*, and *supervised skill practice*. How much of each you'll need depends on your starting point. The first step is to participate in a well-led growth group. In addition, take advantage of all the intensive growth workshops, marathons, and retreats (sponsored by growth centers, by churches, schools, management groups) that you can find. This phase of training has two purposes—continuing your personal growth and learning various styles of group facilitation through experience. How long you'll need as a group member depends on how much growing you have to do. Persons like myself, who are not natural growth facilitators, usually require extensive growth experiences, beginning with some form of depth therapy, to reduce inner blocks to growth.[8]

Step two is the acquiring of a basic understanding of key

concepts in interpersonal and group dynamics, group counseling and therapy, and the human potentials movement. Insights from reading, lectures, and training courses can illuminate and make more functional your growth group experiences.

The third step is practice in co-leading a group with an experienced facilitator, or solo-leading a group under supervision. Tape record sessions (with the group's permission, of course) and play segments of these in supervisory meetings. Supervision in a small group of leaders-in-training is especially valuable, providing as it does both a continuing support/growth group and a place to learn from others' experiences in leading groups.

If you're a clergyman, teacher, youth leader, or other professional, with some competence in counseling, you may decide simply to dive in by leading a group immediately. Many of us have done this with mixed-to-good results. However, the more training and supervision you receive, the better the odds of avoiding major problems and of functioning effectively.

If you are a nonprofessional the three steps are basically the same though they probably will require more time. To maximize your effectiveness as well as minimize the risk of doing harm, continue to use the *backup principle*—i.e., maintain an ongoing consultive relationship with a skilled professional to backup your work with groups. Also, continue in your own growth/support group while you are leading groups. These two suggestions are essential for lay facilitators;[9] they are also sound advice for professional counselors.

SELECTION OF PERSONS TO TRAIN AS FACILITATORS

These criteria can be used in selecting potential facilitators for training:

Is he a loving, non–manipulative person in his relationships?
Is he in touch with his own feelings, including negative ones?

Is he open to new ideas, relationships? (Is he teachable and growing?)
Does he ring true most of the time? (Is he congruent?)
Is his self-esteem firm?
Can he listen to other people? (Is he present?)

One person responded to this list: "That really eliminates me with my can of worms!" Actually, he proved to be an excellent facilitator. What's needed is not a paragon of mental health, without inner conflicts or problems. (If such a person existed, he'd frighten us ordinary mortals). The important thing is that a person possess an appreciable degree of the above characteristics. The greater the degree, the easier it is to train him as a growth facilitator.

If one recruits a growth group, using these criteria, the group experience itself will identify several people who have both the inclination and the aptitudes to lead groups themselves. The natural facilitators who emerge, after some additional training, can become co-leaders of groups while continuing in an ongoing leaders' growth group. This is a practical way of developing a cadre of growth facilitators in an organization or agency.

EVALUATING YOUR GROUPS

To improve your group leadership, approach your groups with an *evaluation perspective.* Devise ways of measuring the relative effectiveness of various selection methods, group formats, and leadership approaches. To supplement verbal evaluations, I often use a simple post-meeting and end-of-group sentence completion form such as this:

In this group, the most helpful things were:
The least helpful things were:
My strongest feelings were:
In future groups I hope that:

A useful group-life checklist allowing participants to rate a group on communication, acceptance of persons, leadership, climate of relationships, and other aspects can be found in Philip Anderson's *Church Meetings that Matter*.[10] Evaluation is not a frill; rather it is essential to discovering what you are accomplishing in groups and how you can do better. If you are interested in objective research on groups, consult the literature.[11]

KEEPING THE ENLIVENER ALIVE

It's not an easy world in which to stay a person—loving, authentic, alive. As a growth-group leader or potential leader, your most difficult and essential resource is yourself. Finding relationships to nurture and re-energize your inner being is crucially important. A growth group is not a place where a leader *does* something *to* the group. It's a shared adventure in relating, one in which the leader *is* something *with* the group in their joint search. To *be* something enlivening is much more difficult than to do something technically appropriate. So, whatever else you do, find at least one nurturing relationship. It's the only way to keep the enlivener alive.

Additional Reading

SMALL GROUP LEADERSHIP:

Gordon, Thomas, *Group-Centered Leadership*. Boston: Houghton Mifflin, 1955.

Kemp, C. Gratton, "The Leader," *Small Groups and Self-Renewal*, New York: Seabury Press, 1971, Chap. 5.

Leslie, Robert C., "Leadership in Sharing Groups," in *Sharing Groups in the Church*. Nashville: Abingdon Press, 1971, Chap. VIII.

Reid, Clyde, "The Leader of the Small Group," in *Groups Alive—Church Alive*. New York: Harper & Row, 1969, Chap. V.

Rogers, Carl R., "Can I Be a Facilitative Person in a Group?" in *Carl Rogers on Encounter Groups*, Harper & Row, 1970, Chapter 3.

AWARENESS TOOLS:

Gunther, Bernard, *Sense Relaxation*. New York: Collier Books, 1968.

Gunther, Bernard, *What to Do Till the Messiah Comes*. New York: Collier Books, 1971.

Lewis, Howard R. and Streitfeld, Harold S. *Growth Games, How to Tune In Yourself, Your Family, Your Friends*. New York: Harcourt Brace Jovanovich, 1970.

Pfeiffer, J. W., and Jones, J. E., *A Handbook of Structured Experiences for Human Relations Training*. Iowa City: University Associates Press, Vols. I, II, and III, 1969, 1970, 1971.

Schutz, William C., *Joy, Expanding Human Awareness*. New York: Grove Press, 1967.

Stevens, John O., *Awareness: exploring, experimenting, experiencing*. Lafayette, Calif.: Real People Press, 1971.

"Encountertapes for Personal Growth Groups." Human Development Institute, Bell and Howell, Atlanta, Ga., 1968.

REFERENCES

1. Carl Rogers, *Carl Rogers on Encounter Groups*, p. 45.

2. Eric Berne, *Games People Play* (New York: Grove Press, 1964).

3. Experiments with so-called "leaderless" encounter groups at the Western Behavioral Sciences Institute employed a series of tape-recorded instructions which groups followed. In a sense, a leader was actually present in the structure and instructions thus provided. The findings of this research showed that in these groups significant changes in persons occurred. Self-help groups (A.A. and others), without trained leaders, achieve rates of social recoveries (restoration to constructive living) which probably surpass those of professionally staffed therapies. A.A. utilizes the extensive structure of "the program," the Big Book, the Twelve Traditions, etc., and natural leadership ability to fulfill leader functions.

4. This study was made by Irvin D. Yalom and Morton A. Lieberman. Subjects (170 Stanford students) who had completed ten-week encounter session showed a 10 percent "casualty" rate, the key to which is the behavior of the leader. "A Study of Encounter Group Casualties," *Archives of General Psychiatry*, 1971.

5. William C. Schutz, *Joy, Expanding Human Awareness*, p. 11.

6. For an illuminating discussion of these points see Arthur Foster, "Exploring Conflict Dynamics through Non-Verbal Communication," *C.T.S. Register*, May, 1969. (Quote from p. 32).

7. What follows is the way I use these exercises. Most of them are not original. They come from many sources and have been adapted and modified. The books by Schutz and Gunther are sources of many of these and others.

8. Persons who are highly constricted by anxiety and inner conflicts, which do not improve substantially with therapy, should find fulfillment in directions other than group leadership.

9. There are risks, of course, in recommending the training of persons without an academic or clinical foundation. But, in my view, the potential gains more than justify the risks (which can be minimized by careful selection and continuing coaching). Lay persons with solid self-esteem acquire facilitator skills rapidly and often make excellent growth group leaders. There is no convincing reason why the talents of these natural growth stimulators should not be used to meet the need for widespread growth opportunities.

10. Philadelphia: United Church Press, 1965, pp. 50-52. A useful "Leader Effectiveness Inventory" can be found in *Discussion: A Guide to Effective Practice* by David Potter and M. P. Anderson (Belmont, Calif.: Wadsworth Pub. Co., 1970, Second Edition, pp. 99-100).

11. See Kemp's *Small Groups and Self-Renewal*, Chap. 9; Ohlsen's *Group Counseling*, Chap. 12; and Rogers' *Carl Rogers on Encounter Groups*, Chap. 7.

CHAPTER 4

Marriage Growth Groups—
Developing Intimacy

The New Marriage offers an ongoing adventure of self-discovery, personal growth, unfoldment, and fulfillment. . . . Growth and the actualizing of personal potential is . . . a joyous and deeply satisfying process which can bring to marriage a new quality of zest for living, of *joie de vivre*, and of excitement.

HERBERT A. OTTO, "The New Marriage"[1]

ON FEBRUARY 9, 1971, the Los Angeles area where we live was hit by a medium-sized earthquake. In one section there was disastrous loss of life and property. The telephone company reported that 1,700,000 more phone calls were made that day into and out of the Los Angeles basin than on a normal Tuesday. This figure represents people reaching out to people. (It doesn't count the tens of thousands who tried to call but couldn't because of jammed lines.) When disaster strikes, we suddenly interrupt our hectic busyness and our preoccupation with less important things and turn to what really matters most—the people we love and who love us. It is with these close relationships that the next five chapters are concerned.

For the vast majority of us, the most promising human contacts for satisfying basic heart hungers are one's marriage partner, children, other family members, and close friends. Marriage can and should be an oasis where growth is nurtured so that we can live responsively and responsibly *in* society. Developing the skills of creative intimacy is the way to make this a reality. If you're married, ask yourself two questions: *Are both you and your spouse satisfied with the general quality of your marriage? Do you like the effects of your relationship on the development of your personal talents and strengths?* If the answer is "No" from either of you to either question, then you should take some positive action to improve your marriage. Marriage-growth or marriage-enrichment groups have helped many couples who wanted more in and from their marriages.

If your marriage is painfully fragmented, a growth approach probably won't help. Instead, marriage counseling or therapy is indicated. But if your marriage is a "tired friendship," not breaking apart but monotonous and dull, or if it is pained and a little empty at times but o.k. and even downright happy at others, a growth group may be precisely what you need to liven things up, improve communication, and increase your times of closeness and joy. Even if there's much you like about your relationship, you're probably using only a fraction of your positive marriage potential. The good news is that any two people with a reasonably firm relationship to build on and a willingness to make the necessary self-investment, can develop a more lively, satisfying marriage. A growth group can be an invaluable resource in this renewal.

That contemporary marriage and the isolated nuclear family are in trouble cannot be denied. (Consider, for a start, the newspaper items on divorce, swingers, communes, women's liberation, and the sex-ethics revolution.) But, in spite of the problems and abundant predictions to the contrary, marriages and families seem to have a future. Gallup pollsters asked 7,948 students at 48 colleges to pick two areas, out of half a dozen, which they thought would be most important to them ten years hence. Eighty-seven percent picked family life as one of the areas.[2] If we can make marriage more fulfilling and zesty, rather than the "dull, deadening drag" which it is for many people, some youth who now prefer alternatives may opt for marriage. One function of growth groups is to help couples cope with marital "future shock" by enabling them to achieve more of the "adventure of self-discovery, personal growth, unfoldment, and fulfillment" in their marriages.

FOUR CRUCIAL GROWTH STAGES

At each marital stage, marriage groups should be readily available to every couple wishing to accelerate their mutual development. Every community should create a network of low-cost groups for at least four types of couples: pre-marrieds (see Chapter 6) early, middle, and older marrieds. Churches, schools, and agencies share the strategic opportunity/responsibility for creating such a growth network. Each stage of marriage has its particular frustrations and satisfactions, its romance, challenges, and needs. One never has it "made" in a marriage. Just when you think things are all set, something changes—a baby is born, a youth leaves the nest, a husband retires—and a whole new set of problems sits like a mountain on what was your smooth marital road. We're different people, to some degree, at each stage; therefore our marriages must change to meet new needs. That's the challenge of marriage. Growth groups, for "normal" marriages, can help us make the most of each new chapter.

LEADING MARRIAGE GROUPS

The principles and methods of leading marriage groups are mainly the same as those described in Chapters 1 to 3. The only basic difference is that a couples group[*] is a group composed of several (pre-established) two-person groups. In contrast to groups of initially unrelated individuals, one is dealing with three to six natural units (couples). There are advantages to this which the leader should utilize in his approach: First, couples bring well-practiced "games" (interaction patterns) to the group. As they automatically demonstrate these patterns in relating in the group, the leader and group members can help them identify patterns which block intimacy and those which hold promise and merit strengthening. Second, the couples can continue their joint growth work between sessions, a major advantage, which home assignments can facilitate. In all growth groups, but particularly in marital groups, significant progress often comes between sessions. Third, couples often continue, after a group's termination, to work toward the growth goals they selected during the group sessions. The goal of a marriage group is to help each marriage become an ongoing two-person growth group. Because of these factors, we find marriage groups especially satisfying to lead. Furthermore, the knowledge that couples are the "architects of the family" (Satir), gives marriage groups a special importance for the future.

In our experience, four to six couples is the optimal size and six to eight weeks the minimal length. An initial all-day or Friday night-Saturday session is a major asset.

Growth-work within marriage groups has three foci: develop-

---

[*] Some leaders of marriage therapy groups prefer to have husbands and wives in separate groups. In *growth* groups, where the purpose is to provide opportunity for couples to strengthen their interaction, it is logical and much more efficient to see the whole relationship. To directly observe a couple relating allows the leader and group to be more helpful to them in their efforts to communicate and relate effectively. Having couples together gives them an opportunity actually to practice the new skills *in* the group. Occasional sessions without both spouses can produce understanding of how their ways of relating may be blocking each other's growth at points.

ing each individual's talents; nurturing of each couple's relationship; being growth-agents, couple-to-couple. An experienced growth facilitator reports that in the "Marriage Effectiveness" weekends which he and his wife co-lead, they have found it important to balance the emphasis on nurture and handling conflict constructively.[3] Focusing only on love-support-nurture makes marital groups one-sided and increasingly irrelevant to real relationships which inevitably blend love and conflict.

Dealing frankly with the longing of couples for more mutual pleasuring in their sex life is a vital function of marriage groups. In most marriages, if the general relationship is dull, frozen, or hostile, sex will be too. As couples learn how to lower the walls between them by better communication and the use of conflict-resolution skills, they will enjoy reconnecting in many ways—from sensual to spiritual—often in the same experiences. In a growing marriage, sex is a delicious source of renewal and self-esteem, allowing couples to experience the amazing unifying of themselves and their love in sex play and joining. As a group member who had rediscovered this said (quoting a best seller on sex): "It's 'one of the few really beautiful and satisfying experiences in this world that isn't taxed!' "[4]

Male/female co-leaders, giving both perspectives on issues, are particularly suited to marriage groups. The importance of this type of leadership has become clearer with the rise of the new consciousness among women. Having a leader of each sex stimulates growth work. An added advantage is husband/wife co-leadership, provided their relationship is open and growing.

A GROUP FOR YOUNG MARRIEDS

For four months, six young couples, married less than five years, met two hours weekly with two mini-marathons (extended sessions of six hours each). My wife and I were co-facilitators. These couples were in the "establishment stage" of the family life cycle, a strategic time when lifelong patterns of marital relating (or not relating) are learned.

Group interaction centered at various times on each of the three demanding skills which many married young adults struggle to acquire: *husbanding/wifing skills; vocational skills;* and *parenting skills.* Marriage issues were central to the discussions, but the other two themes were frequently interwoven. The claims of jobs (and graduate school) versus their hunger for more time alone together, were often considered by the group. Couples with children focused on resolving conflicts about discipline and parental roles. In the pre-Christmas session, there was vigorous discussion of forthcoming visits to parents' homes and the marriage conflicts likely to be triggered by these meetings. This raised a crucial issue facing most young adults—the risk of "letting go" of the dependence on parents as emotional need-satisfiers, so that, as couples, they may commit themselves to meeting their own major needs in marriage.

One man, having trouble breaking a parental tie, knew his anger sprang from feelings of deprivation of love as a child. He was invited to "talk with his father" whom he was to fantasize as sitting in the empty chair in front of him. (A Gestalt therapy method.) A torrent of painful, conflicted feelings flowed; as these were experienced and talked through, there seemed to be a release of tension in his struggle for inner liberation.

The teaching function of a growth group usually evolved as members and leaders reflected on their experiences together. In an early session, for example, one husband repeatedly blocked communication by "coming on like big daddy" (as his wife put it heatedly). After they had worked awhile on their interaction, my wife described Berne's Parent-Adult-Child system as a technique for couples to use in halting their Parent-Child games and mobilizing their Adult sides. We reviewed the TA system briefly (Chapter 3), giving an illustration from our own marriage. Then I asked: "Can you see any Parent-Child games in your marriages?" Several couples gave examples from their relationships. A discussion followed concerning their use of TA to help themselves. In subsequent sessions, TA was often mentioned by couples as they experimented with it in their families.

We encouraged everyone (individually and jointly as couples) to formulate personal and marital growth goals toward which they would work. In early sessions, couples talked mainly about conflicts and problems. Gradually they began to spend more of the sessions discussing positive goals including things they "had always wanted to do." In early sessions, couples talked mainly about themselves and their relationship. As the group trust level rose, they not only began to share much more frankly about their own marriages, they also began to confront each other about Parent-Child games and unused assets.

As part of the closing session, each person told what he had learned in the group and how he intended to use this in working on his marriage. My wife commented during the closing group evaluation that it made us feel pleased (as well as slightly jealous) to see them communicating at a level, after a few years together, that it had taken us much longer to reach in our marriage.

A MARRIAGE ENRICHMENT WORKSHOP

This "Marriage Enrichment" workshop involved twenty-four couples—a few early marrieds, the majority middle marrieds, and a substantial number of older marrieds. It met mornings, afternoons, and evenings, for four and a half days using college facilities. These ingredients went into each day's program:

Input Session: (9:00 to 10:20 A.M.) Dialogue between the co-leaders and with the couples. General theme—"The Care and Feeding of a Growing Marriage." Specific topics chosen on the basis of participants' interests.

Lab Session: (10:45 to 12:00 A.M.) Used for demonstrating and practicing communication skills, awareness exercises, conflict-resolution, role-playing, etc. For example, after an input session on
communication, the co-leaders listened and responded to each
other's feelings. Then, in groups of two couples, everyone practiced empathic listening and "checking out" ("Let's see if I'm hear-
ing what you're feeling . . .").

Self-Other Awareness: (1:15 to 2:10 P.M.) A launching session for the
whole group using awareness exercises with couples to awaken
feelings which could be worked through in small groups. Exercises
which proved to be fruitful included: Trust jogging, making a
joint collage, non-verbal communication, Indian wrestling, sharing
pain, and finishing the sentences addressed to each other "I want
from you . . ." and "I appreciate in you . . ."

Marriage Growth Groups: (2:15 to 4:15 P.M., with a mini-marathon
the third day, 2:15 to 9:15 P.M.) Each group had six couples
and a leader. In the final evaluation, many participants rated these
groups as the most valuable part of the workshop.

After the first evening, couples were asked to discuss and write
out a list of "The Strengths and Assets in Our Marriage," to be
shared in their growth groups, if they chose. For some couples,
working together on this statement involved more reflection on
their positive potentials than they had ever done before.

Because many of the couples were middle-aged, the concerns
of that life-stage were discussed frequently, both in input
sessions and growth groups. These included—how to deepen
a marriage relationship neglected during frantic child-rearing,
getting-ahead years; maintaining self-esteem in the midst of
increasing evidence of aging; coping with stresses of "adolescing
children"; dependency and death of parents; menopause; the
emptying nest; wives' need to develop new satisfactions as
children leave. Considerable consensus emerged on ways of making the most of the mid-years (and beyond) of marriage: finding

time to continue courtship, working through conflicts, deepening communication; learning to "own" oneself, that is, taking responsibility for developing one's own potentialities; turning off the inner Parent (caught between two dependent generations) so that the Child sides can play regularly; finding a faith that makes adult sense and is functional for facing the second half of life; finding a cause that matters outside the marriage.

The older couples in the workshop dealt with some of their stresses and concerns in the growth groups. One couple facing the husband's imminent retirement struggled with the feelings and practical decisions this would bring. One couple told of developing some rich new relationships in a sharing group at their church; this led to a discussion of how older persons can cope with the loneliness and grief of repeated loss. Several couples described the satisfactions they were receiving from volunteer service programs ("volunteer grandparents" in children's institutions, for instance) which allowed them to keep involved and to use skills acquired over the years.

In the closing evaluation session, people were invited to tell what they planned to do as a result of the workshop. One of the significant outcomes was the decision, on the part of several couples, to find or set up ongoing growth-support groups in their own areas. Experiencing the juicy taste of depth relationships had made them want more of what one person called a "clan-in-the-spirit" for mutual fellowship and growth.

A LEADERLESS GROWTH GROUP

A church-sponsored young couples group, which had been meeting monthly for over a year for informal fellowship, decided to meet as a leaderless growth group, one and a half hours on each of six consecutive Friday evenings. The seven couples in the group included three individuals who had had previous growth group experience. These persons became de facto facilitators. The group chose a book on marriage[5] and agreed to read two chapters between sessions as a stimulus to interaction.

The group succeeded in reaching a feeling level, discussing such matters as their perceptions of each other, feelings about having children as this relates to marital intimacy, and the grief experience of one member. There seemed to be a consensus that the group was helpful to the participants.

MAKING MARRIAGE A GROWTH GROUP

Experiences in a group are most likely to help a marriage become an ongoing stimulus to growth if these guidelines are observed: (1) The couple agrees on certain things both want (goals) and decides how to attain them (strategy). They tell the group about both goals and strategy. (2) Each partner concentrates on changing his side of the relationship rather than trying to reform the other. (3) Between group sessions they use new communication and problem-solving skills learned in the group.

Marriage is very much what we as couples make it. We construct what it becomes, day by day, as we argue and love, have intercourse, take out the garbage, hurt and pleasure each other, raise children and search for meanings, make little and big decisions, feed the relationship by caring, or starve it by neglect. By our dozens of daily "growth choices" (Maslow) we can create a living relationship. It's as simple and as complex as that.

From the ups and downs of our own growth struggles over the years, this truth becomes ever clearer and more of a challenge: "Marriage could provide the ideal setting for personal development. It could open the way to lifelong learning."[6]

Creative closeness in marriage is like a many-faceted diamond. Most of us polish only a few areas and leave the others rough. However far you've gone in achieving intimacy, it's safe to say there are other aspects which could be developed if you worked on them. A growth group can give you that fresh approach to developing a more satisfying marriage.

Additional Reading—Marriage Growth Groups

("L" = of interest primarily to group leaders.)

L   Ackerman, N. W., *The Psychodynamics of Family Life*. New York: Basic Books, 1958.

Bach, George R., and Wyden, Peter, *The Intimate Enemy: How to Fight Fair in Love and Marriage*. New York: William Morrow, 1969.

Baruch, D. W., and Miller, Hyman, *Sex in Marriage, New Understandings*. New York: Harper & Row, 1962.

Berne, Eric, *Games People Play, the Psychology of Human Relationships*. New York: Grove Press, 1964. Chap. 7 describes marital games.

Clinebell, Howard J., Jr. and Charlotte H., *The Intimate Marriage*. New York: Harper & Row, 1970. Annotated bibliography.

Eichenlaub, John E., *New Approaches to Sex in Marriage*. New York: Dell Books, 1968.

Gunther, Bernard, *Sense Relaxation*. New York: Collier Books, 1968, Chapter 9, "Intimate Games."

Otto, Herbert, *More Joy in Your Marriage*. New York: Hawthorne Books, 1968.

Snyder, Ross, *Inscape, Discovering Personhood in the Marriage Relationship*. Nashville: Abingdon Press, 1968.

L   Stewart, Charles W., *The Minister as Marriage Counselor*. Nashville: Abingdon Press, rev. ed., 1970, Chap. XII, "Group Marriage Counseling."

Tournier, Paul, *To Understand Each Other*. Richmond, Va.: John Knox Press, 1967.

REFERENCES

1. "Marriage as a Framework for Developing Personal Potential," *The Family In Search of a Future*, Herbert A. Otto, Ed., New York: Appleton-Century-Crofts, 1970, p. 113.

2. Gallup Poll, *Los Angeles Times*, February 11, 1971.

3. Personal communication, Kenneth Jones, Corvallis, Ore., February 10, 1971.

4. *The Sensuous Woman*, "J" (New York: Dell Publishing Co., 1969), p. 15.

5. Howard and Charlotte Clinebell, *The Intimate Marriage*.

6. George B. Leonard, "The Man and Woman Thing," *Look*, December 24, 1968, p. 57.

CHAPTER 5

Women's (and Men's)
Liberation Groups

The pedestal upon which women have been placed has all too often, upon closer inspection, been revealed as a cage.

RAYMOND E. PETERS, Associate Justice,
California Supreme Court[1]

Women in our society are still trained from infancy to entertain, to please, and to serve—mainly men. Women are not yet raised to be just people—whole, fully participating individuals.

JOANNE COOKE, *The New Woman*[2]

OF ALL OUR SOCIETY's multiple revolutions, the revolution in female/male consciousness and roles will become the most earth-shaking; eventually it will touch and change every aspect of man-woman relationships.

No marriage (or premarriage) growth group can be "with it" today and avoid grappling with the issues raised by the women's liberation movement. Growth groups exist, we have said, to develop human potential, nurture self-esteem, and enliven persons in their relationships. *These are also implicit goals of women's*

71

liberation! Think of the wasted intelligence, leadership capacity, creativity, strength, and sensitivity of the millions of women denied full educational and vocational opportunities, kept in narrow role-boxes, using only a fraction of their capacities!

Anthropologist Margaret Mead holds that changes now occurring in women's roles are as radical as those which hit men some 14,000 years ago—when agriculture was first practiced. After eons of scrambling for sustenance as wandering hunters, men started to raise enough food to permit some free time (which made possible the eventual development of culture). The roles of women, however, remained largely unchanged—bearing and rearing children, doing housework, and serving men. Now, with population pressures reducing family size and with extended longevity, women generally will not be able to find fulfillment in homemaking roles alone.[3] (Not that these roles ever did really foster the full self-realization of many women.) Women in increasing numbers are awakening to this fact and to the continuing oppression of a male-dominated society. There is a mounting insistence among women (including many who reject the methods of militant liberationists) that they be treated as full human beings, with freedom to choose and to develop their personal gifts and abilities. As psychologist Naomi Weisstein declares: "Women's liberation is part of a movement toward a just and humane society, a society in which no human being will be forced into a servant role."[4]

The changing consciousness of women has already begun to precipitate what will become a massive crisis in marriage. Those of us who do marriage counseling can think of examples of marital conflicts stemming from a three-way collision among a wife's need for fulfillment, a husband's need to be one-up, and the needs of both for a satisfying marriage.

Growth groups can help both women and men discover the creative possibilities that lie in the profound changes ahead. *The*

new femininity offers opportunities for (in fact demands) a richer
masculinity; together men and women can create more mutually
humanizing relationships, including more delightful marriages,
than have been possible before. Women's liberation can mean
"human liberation."

The awakening of feminine awareness will reach into marriages
at all stages. For those couples who have the mutual caring, imagination and guts to struggle through to new ways of relating, a
more satisfying companionship-marriage can result. The Parent/
Child distancing games which have devitalized one-up/one-down
marriages, can be replaced by the intimacy of a growing
Adult-to-Adult relationship.[5] For these fortunate couples the coming crisis in marriage will be a crisis of growth!

TYPES OF FEMALE/MALE LIBERATION GROUPS

Marital and premarital growth groups should deal explicitly and
personally with how changing roles affect the participants. This
will happen spontaneously (which is best), if there's even one
"liberated" woman present; she'll be sensitized to the innumerable
put-downs all women experience (but many are resigned to). In
one way or another, she'll confront the men with the prejudices,
subtle and not-so-subtle, with which most men are infected. She'll
also confront acquiescent women.

In addition to dealing with liberation issues in mixed groups,
special women-only groups are needed *to provide mutual help in*
changing self-defeating attitudes toward themselves (consciousness raising), coping with the conflicts and challenges of the
struggle for full personhood, and working for liberation through
social action. (Several thousand women's liberation groups
already operate in North America.) Men-only groups may become useful in coping with distinctively male pressures and
problems associated with the revolution in roles. But, as those in
the power position, most males have little motivation to work on

their side of the relationship unless they are confronted by the "victims." All-women groups can be good preparation for men-women groups, where both sexes can discuss and discover mutually fulfilling relationships.

To help couples develop more liberating relationships, the leader must be aware of the vital human issues involved and aware of his or her own prejudices. We're surrounded by our culture as fish are by water; it's impossible to grow up in a sex-prejudiced culture without catching some of it. In the self-image of males it takes the form of a feeling of superiority to women; in females it expresses itself in the feeling that one is worthwhile only in relation to a man or men. To be a *facilitator of liberation,* a leader must work to change these prejudgments and be sensitive to the person-damaging social forces which the liberation movement is fighting.

A WOMEN'S LIBERATION GROUP

The specific objectives of an all-women growth group depends, of course, on the wants, needs, and unused gifts of its individual members. There are, however, common directions in which many women desire to move. The following is from a "Personal Enrichment Group" composed of women (late thirties and early forties):

Joan: "I really can't get excited about women's lib . . . not for me . . . My kids are about out of the nest. Liberation is just around the corner for me . . . good years to use as I want."

Betty: "But what *do* you want—for the next twenty years or so?"

Joan: "I don't really know at this point. What can you do with an ancient B.A. in English?"

Betty: "When I think of spending even the next five years volunteering 'til I'm blue in the face, entertaining Dan's clients, bridge club and church things (she scowls) . . . I've got to find something that uses more of me, I guess . . . not necessarily a job . . . but something I *really* want to do with me. I've had it up to here (points to chin) with all decisions depending on Dan's career . . . Where do *I* come in?"

Betty's honesty about her frustrations and her need to find another dimension to her life triggered brisk sharing in the group. Later in the session—

Joan: "I've toyed with the idea of seeing if I could get a master's in rehab therapy. I like the volunteer things I do with the handicapped. But I haven't been near a classroom in almost twenty years and . . . well, I wasn't exactly a brain in college—interested mostly in trapping a man, I guess. I doubt if I could make it—with all these bright young things."

Leader: "Have you considered taking a course at the state university to see how it goes? Lots of women commute for a course or two."

Joan: "I've thought of that. Even mentioned it to Tom [her husband]. He wasn't exactly thrilled. He asked why I don't spend more time with my volunteer groups, if I want to work with the handicapped. He seemed to feel that it would be a reflection on him for me to have a career."

Leader: "How do you feel about that?"

Joan: "A little put down, I guess, and hurt at the time . . . Of course, a part of me agrees with Tom. As he says, we don't particularly need the extra money. But I've tried lots of volunteer things. They're good but . . . well, they still don't really satisfy me. Maybe they should . . ."

What must Joan do to free and use more of her capabilities? First, she must *decide on goals*. What does she really want to do with the next twenty years? What is feasible? Second, she must *devise workable plans*. A career guidance center may provide aptitude testing and educational advice to help her check the realism of her goals and strategies. If she sets her sights on becoming a rehabilitation therapist, where can she get training?

If Joan's growth goals require enlarging her orbit beyond home and volunteer activities, she will have to do two other things— *overcome her low self-estimate* regarding competing "in the world," and *cope with her husband's resistance* to changes in their roles. The group's perceptions of her abilities and resourcefulness, shared in subsequent sessions, helped to rectify her "I'm-o.k.-only-in-'female'-roles" feelings. The group also challenged her to take the leap—at the risk of possible failure—by enrolling in one course to test and toughen flabby academic muscles. For strengthening self-esteem, nothing succeeds like success. That B+ did wonders for her self-image as a person with brains she could use in a graduate program if she chose.

Before enrolling in the course, Joan reopened with her husband the issue of her role for the next twenty years. A stormy session ensued. When the smoke cleared, Joan explained that she valued their marriage and loved him but that she had to start liking *herself* more. To do this, she pointed out, might or might not involve a career, in addition to her present role. "What I need is the freedom to discover what is best for me and you and the children." Tom expressed his desire for her to be happy and fulfilled as a person but showed continuing distress at the thought of things changing as they would if she acquired a career. They eventually reached agreement on Joan's plans to take a course on a trial basis.

Obviously Joan and Tom have a considerable way to go toward renegotiating their relationship so that *both* will be more fulfilled. Without a new mutually acceptable agreement, their marriage will become increasingly strained. If Joan gives up her search for a revised identity, resentment of her restricted options will escalate. If she goes ahead against his adamant opposition, or if Tom merely gives in, his anger will mount, driving a deeper wedge between them. But, if they can achieve a *revised covenant* —a mutual agreement concerning their roles and needs—their marriage can prosper in fresh ways. A couples' growth group, including others facing the mid-years identity crisis, could help Tom and Joan in their struggles for a new relationship.

A women's growth group should provide activities directed at both *inner liberation* (raising self-esteem) and *outer liberation* (achieving equal opportunities for women in all areas of society). Women, like blacks and members of other oppressed groups, must break their inner bondage and gain self-esteem if they are to use fully their potential in collective efforts to change the systems of injustice (discriminatory laws, pay scales, admissions policies to professional schools, among others).

Unconsciously, most women have adopted the attitudes of our culture, viewing themselves as naturally subordinate. This is described in women's liberation as "the enemy within." Long dependence and semivoluntary servitude have produced ambivalence toward the risks and responsibilities of freedom. Prejudices toward women professionals *among women* reflect their low self-esteem *as women* (even though these persons may be confident and competent in their "feminine" roles). Consciousness-raising in groups reverses this negative conditioning, helping women "take pride and delight in our femaleness . . . trust and love each other as sisters (not competitors for male approval) . . . deciding and re-deciding each day, individually and together, that we will take control over our lives . . . and struggle together for the liberation of all women."[6] This is the new feminine consciousness which can be nurtured in a liberation growth group.

In addition to growth-action groups focused explicitly on "women's liberation," a variety of all-women growth groups organized around other objectives should be available, e.g., "Women's Sharing Group," "Enrichment Group," "Women in a Changing

World." Thus, many women who "wouldn't be caught dead" in a women's liberation meeting can have the opportunity to deal with the issues which inevitably will confront them as sex roles change in our society.

Women who are awakened to their full femininity and to liberation issues are most effective as leaders of women's groups. Couples or other male/female co-leaders who have been involved with these issues are best suited to this dimension of marital group work. Unless a man is unusually liberated from male prejudice and empathetic regarding the experience of being a woman in our culture, he had better not attempt to lead an all-women liberation group.

THE LIBERATION THRUST IN MIXED GROUPS

In the fabric of human existence, the lives of men and women are inextricably interwoven—sexually, biologically, emotionally, socially. Neither can be truly free or fulfilled unless *both* are, because each enriches and completes the other's world. It is in men-women groups that women's liberation can most fully become human liberation.

Mixed groups can *awaken both sexes quickly and personally to the issues.* One or more sensitized women will feel the pain of male put-downs; they can respond by confronting the man or men responsible with the effects of their behavior. Couples often recognize one-up/one-down games more quickly in other relationships than in their own. Furthermore, mixed groups *provide both stimulus and support* for couples to grow jointly around the crunch of changing roles. It's not easy to change a marriage in any basic way. A group provides both caring *support* and caring *confrontation*—the constructive pressure for a couple not to settle for less than they can achieve. It's in the actual give-and-take of interacting that couples work (or muddle) through to more fulfilling patterns.

GAINS FOR MEN IN WOMEN'S LIBERATION

In liberated marriages and other male/female relationships, men *lose* their feelings of superiority, control, economic advantage, and the practical satisfactions of a servant-satellite relationship. In growth groups, men should discover what they can *gain* as well. *Deeper companionship* is one. There's a mutuality based on equality that can't be present in any up/down relationship. *A wife has more to give* because she feels more adequate and has a richer life. There is *less mutual manipulating* which creates I-it feelings between people. Inequality breeds manipulation—overt domination by the husband; sneaky, "feminine" controlling by the wife. *Increased sexual pleasuring* is another gain for both men and women. A woman who feels worthwhile and free to enjoy being a woman is great in bed! Contrast this with the "frozen anger"[7] of women who feel chronically inferior.

Another gain for a man is *knowing that he is involved in the fulfillment, rather than the exploitation, of another human being*. Still another benefit may be a *fuller sharing by the wife of responsibility for family support*. As a group member put it: "Maybe fewer of us men will kick off at forty with heart attacks and booze, when we let our wives carry more of the load." *Freedom to feel* the rich range of human emotions, with no off-limits categories labeled "unmasculine" is another gain. Those of us who were taught in our early years that "little boys don't cry" (or feel tenderness, or admit needing others, etc.) have a new chance to enrich our inner lives. The freedom to *be*, for women, and the freedom to feel, for men, are two sides of a liberated relationship. *Greater closeness to children* is another gain. One couple renegotiated and actually rewrote their marriage contract, dividing rights and duties evenly, including caring for their small daughter. After several months under the new agreement, she said to her father one day, "You know, Daddy, I used to love Mommy more than you, but now I love you both the same."[8]

LIBERATION AWARENESS EXERCISES

Here are some of the group methods we have used to stimulate awareness of liberation issues. At a one-day intimacy workshop focused on changing roles, (for about 60 couples), my wife and I began by dialoguing on the emerging shapes of marriage (including ours) and the new possibilities for conflict and intimacy therein. Then, volunteers from the audience role-played a mid-years marriage involved in head-on collision between the wife's intense desire to complete her college course and the husband's equally intense desire for them to go for a business and pleasure fling in Las Vegas (during her examination week). This role-playing took workshop participants to the feelings-attitudes level of changing roles almost immediately. The debriefing, in small groups, was intense and personal.

The following exercise awakens awareness of liberation issues by heightening polarization:[9]

Fishbowl technique—Men sit in the center and discuss how they really feel about women drivers (doctors, clergy, lib-ers, etc.). Then the women, who have observed from an outer circle, report on what they heard. Following this, women sit in the middle circle and discuss ways they feel put-down in a male-oriented society, after which the men report and interaction continues in a single circle.

THE STAKES ARE HIGH

A revolution in human relations is like an earthquake—it shakes everything; even strong structures feel the effects and shaky ones collapse. The stakes are very high. A research psychologist[10] reports that a major concentration of mental health problems in our country is among women between thirty-five and sixty—women with unused capacities, victims of purposelessness. Statistics on divorce, swinging (spouse-swapping), multiple sex, Kinsey's revelations on rates of infidelity—not to mention the plethora of dull, lifeless, and grim marriages—all point to the fact that run-of-the-mill monogamy is not flourishing. Only an "intensified monogamy," a more total relationship, more "marital spice" and space, and more lusty enjoyment of sex can make monogamy a viable, fulfilling pattern for women and men. Marriages growing toward liberation, toward Adult-to-Adult relationships, can achieve this kind of depth intimacy.

Henrik Ibsen has an interchange in his play, *A Doll's House* (written in 1879), which states pointedly the central issue in women's liberation:

Helmer: Before all else you are a wife and a mother.

Nora: That I no longer believe. I believe that before all else I am a human being just as you are—or at least that I should try to become one.[11]

Additional Reading—Liberation Groups

Bird, Caroline, *Born Female—Source Book for the Women's Lib Movement.* New York: McKay, 1970.

Callahan, Sidney C., *The Illusion of Eve, Modern Women's Quest for Identity.* New York: Sheed and Ward, 1965.

Cooke, Joanne, Bunch-Weeks, Charlotte, and Morgan, Robin, Eds. *The New Woman.* Greenwich, Conn.: Fawcett Publications, 1969.

Doely, Sarah B., *Women's Liberation and the Church.* New York: Association Press, 1970.

Stambler, Sookie, Compiler. *Women's Liberation, Blueprint for the Future.* New York: Ace books, 1970.

REFERENCES

1. From a statement made in declaring a "protective" female employment law discriminatory and unconstitutional. *Los Angeles Times,* Part I, p. 3.

2. J. Cooke, C. Bunch-Weeks, R. Morgan, Eds., *The New Woman, A Motive Anthology*, p. 16.

3. Lecture, N.Y.C. Conference on Values in Psychotherapy, November, 1969.

4. Diane Monk, "Defining the New Feminists," *Los Angeles Times,* January 4, 1970, Sec. I, p. 17.

5. Eric Berne observed that girls are taught to use their Child side to hook the Parent side of males. Thus Parent/Child manipulations tend to dominate many marriages. By subordinating women, our society forces them to use their Child side to get what they want and need. A woman's inner Parent is activated in rearing her children and pampering or nagging her husband. When children leave home, she is reduced to Child/Parent and Parent/Child interaction with her husband, which cannot give her (or him) the human fulfillment they need.

6. Joanne Cooke, et al., *The New Women,* p. 190.

7. My wife has observed that the term "frigidity" often refers to this frozen anger.

8. Alix Shulman, "A Marriage Agreement," *Women's Liberation, A Blueprint for the Future* (New York: Ace Books, 1970), p. 217.

9. For an exercise involving a questionnnaire which elicits basic male/female attitudinal barriers, see Pfeiffer and Jones, *A Handbook of Structured Experience for Human Relations Training* (Iowa City: University Associates Press, 1971), Vol. III, p. 73.

10. Personal communication, Douglas H. Heath, Psychology Department, Haverford College.

11. From the Introduction to *The New Women.*

CHAPTER 6

Youth Growth Groups—
Identity Formation

"It's so exciting! Sensitivity breaks down barriers and you feel emotions unknown by most to even exist. There is such humanness and love in it . . . Sensitivity breaks down all walls. There is no feeling of color, age, or sex. We enter the experience black and white, and young and old, and leave as one human, loving body. I wish more people could be 'turned on' to sensitivity. I've found myself happier since I discovered this type of warmth and love. I can get really high on nature, books, music, and most of all—people. It's beautiful!"

Comments of a high school girl[1]

THESE WORDS of a high school senior describe her experiences in a growth group led by her pastor. They illustrate, with refreshing enthusiasm, the power of the people dynamic to awaken youth to the richness of existence. No age group is more concerned than youth about finding and fulfilling themselves. No age segment of a community can use growth groups more productively.

Adolescence is a time of coming alive—to oneself, to peers, to the wider world of nature and spirit. It's an exciting, confusing, and lonely period for many, especially in these chaotic times. But in all kinds of circumstances, the inward flowering of sexuality

83

occurs. It happened, and beautifully, to a girl, age fourteen, hiding with her family in an Amsterdam loft from the tyranny of a hate state:

The sun is shining, the sky is a deep blue, there is a lovely breeze and I'm longing—so longing—for everything . . . I believe that it's spring within me, I feel that spring is awakening, I feel it in my whole body and soul. It is an effort to behave normally . . . I only know that I am longing.[2]

The search for vivid experiencing—for turning on through rock music, mysticism, drugs, sex, freer relationships with people— is a powerful drive in youth. Because growth groups are an effective method of turning on *to people,* they have a special attraction and usefulness for youth.

Every community, through its churches, schools, community agencies, and youth organizations (the "Y" and others) should provide a smorgasbord of growth opportunities for youth. Few if any investments of group leadership can pay more lasting dividends—nurturing the family builders of the future and, through them, increasing the wholeness of tomorrow's children.

GROUPS AND THE GROWTH OF YOUTH

It is illuminating, both for group leaders and members, to understand how growth groups can meet the particular needs of youth. Here are some of the ways:

Growth groups can help youth achieve a firm, functional identity. Identity formation—"the process of coming to terms with what it means to be a person in one's own right"[3]—is the task facing every adolescent. At the end of a group, one girl said: "I know *me* better now and it feels good."

Groups help youth develop new relationship skills within a lifestyle of interdependence. In groups, high school and college youth "try on for size" better ways of communicating and relating. Bill, a sensitive sixteen-year-old, learned, midway through a sharing group, that his parents were divorcing. Reeling from the blow, he haltingly told the group that his first thought was, "I won't tell the group . . . too much, man . . . they don't need to know." Then, the realization hit him, "Hell, if I ever needed a place where I could spill my guts, this is it." Responding with warmth and concern, the group helped Bill release his hurt, angry feelings, then helped him sort out the pieces—what he could and couldn't do something about.

There is an epidemic of disillusionment, loneliness, and despair among youth.[4] Learning to turn *toward* people, rather than away, when the roof caves in, is part of the answer. Knowing how to use and enjoy a mutual support group is a lifelong asset in a society of massive loneliness.

Growth groups can help youth increase their feelings of self-worth. Behind the know-it-all assertiveness of some youth (which threatens and galls adults) and the shy withdrawal of others, the same gnawing feeling usually lurks: "I'm not sure who I am or how to handle these powerful inner urges or whether I can make it in the mixed-up, demanding world of adulthood." What am I worth? is a central question in youth's identity search. Growth groups let youth experience an affirming community. The group enhances self-esteem by caring enough to really listen, to comfort and to confront. It helps increase self-acceptance by reducing the burden of guilt which many youth carry. It does this by creating a climate of acceptance—of feelings and impulses (around which irrational guilt often forms)—and by confronting the young person with the need to change irresponsible, self-other hurting behavior (the source of appropriate guilt).

Growth groups can help youth learn how to keep their Adult sides in the driver's seat. A growth group can help persons at any age avoid letting the inner Child take over at inappropriate times (often a crucial issue for adolescents).

Ralph: (age 15) "Man, I'm going to be an ecology lawyer—give it to
    these damn polluters!"
Pete: (age 17) "Good show! But how does that fit with the goofin'
    off in school bit?"

Without knowing it, Pete is practicing reality therapy. He's asking
Ralph's inner Adult, "Does what you're doing now lead to where
you want to be?" Ralph's Adult may decide to take over control
from his Child and try to pass the courses because this will move
him toward his goal.

*Groups can help youth prize their own sexuality and affirm that
of others.* Sexuality—maleness and femaleness—is big and important to nearly everyone. It's particularly powerful and pervasive in the consciousness of youth. Much of the moodiness, des-
pondency, and inferiority feelings of even well-adjusted teens are
linked to anxiety and guilt about sexual fantasies, impulses, behavior, and "will-I-be-attractive-enough-to-the-other-sex" worries.
If the leader is affirmative of his or her own sexuality, a group can
provide the first opportunity most youth have had to resolve
hangups in this area.

Prizing oneself as a whole person necessarily includes discovering and liking oneself as a sexual being. Many youth are searching
for their sexual identity, which is difficult when sex roles are
changing so rapidly. They're struggling to connect sex to things
like self-esteem and caring relationships, a difficult assignment in
our fouled-up, sex-saturated society. Growth groups can help. The
ability to celebrate one's sexuality and enjoy one's sexual powers in
pro-people ways increases through completion of the growth tasks
of each stage from infancy through adulthood. Groups can help
youth work through their feelings and attitudes toward sex. When
sex is best (most satisfying and pleasurable) it's in a relationship
of mutual esteem, responsibility, and caring.

Groups can be a launching pad toward adulthood. To enter

adulthood, youth must free themselves from inner dependency ties to parents. To do this, young people need supportive relationships —far enough removed from the source of their childhood attitudes commitments, and values—to evaluate these and help them decide which they can honestly incorporate into their developing adult identity. Youth growth groups can provide such relationships, which become a launching pad for making it into adult orbit. Through the "new family" of the peer group, inner freedom and identity can develop.

Groups provide opportunities for new relationships with adults. If the adult leader is nonjudgmental, caring, and a listener, most youth will communicate openly about what matters to them. To communicate with a trusted nonparent adult, during the period of necessary separation from parents, is affirming to youth in their identity quest. In the family I know best, a creative, open minister was this kind of meaningful adult friend to its teen-age members. Through gangs, cliques, clubs, and steady couple relationships, youth create their own "new families" in which growth occurs. Formal groups supplement these in important ways, including the opportunities for new relationships with adults.

Groups can help youth develop a philosophy that works for them. Functional values and commitments are essential to identity formation. Many youth are searching for ways to make their lives count in our value-conflicted world. The late Abraham Maslow, a growth-oriented psychologist, declared:

Self-actualizing people are, without one single exception, involved in a cause outside their own skin. . . . They are devoted, working at something which is very precious to them—some calling or vocation in the old, priestly sense . . . which they love, so that the work-joy dichotomy in them disappears. . . . All, in one way or another, devote lives to the search for what I have called the 'being values,' the ultimate values which . . . cannot be reduced to anything more ultimate . . . including the truth and beauty and goodness of the ancients.[5]

Millions of youth have rejected as inadequate the values of their parents like money and "getting ahead"; they're searching for "being" values. Witness their efforts to apply the love ethic and to save the planet *for people*. Most youthful cynics are still hoping there may be a way to save mankind from self-pollution and self-destruction.

Growth groups can enable youth to connect with vertical reality. Most youth hunger for what Maslow called "peak experiences." Drugs have allure partly because they offer instant transcendence. The high school girl quoted at the opening of this chapter compared her experiences with marijuana and a growth-in-sensitivity group:

> "Sensitivity is not only as good as marijuana because you can experience fulfillment of emotions, but it is far better. It is not against the law and it has a more lasting effect . . . when it is over and you 'come down' from your sensitivity experience, you have the feeling with you for a long time, whereas with marijuana, when you 'come down' it is depressing."

A vital function of growth groups for all ages is to help people break out of "the heavies" and experience "little moments of ecstasy"—in playfulness, joy, celebration, worship, deep sharing, mystery, and pain. These precious moments can't be manufactured; they happen spontaneously in effective groups. The moment of growth, when the group witnesses an awakening, is such a peak. Religious symbols may be the most appropriate response (though not necessarily). A church youth group embraced as a group and broke into a rousing folk hymn. Another youth group let out a roof-raising cheer of sheer joy. Peak experiences are much more than emotional "trips." They're moments of standing on holy ground, when the group is one with each other and with Life. They are an essential dimension and source of empowering for growth. They are moments of connecting with the Source.

VARIETIES OF YOUTH GROWTH GROUPS

Here are a few of the many types of youth growth groups which have been effective:

Self-discovery group: A counseling minister drew two small groups from his youth fellowships. Some joined as a result of an open invitation. Others—known by the minister to have growth problems—received individual invitations. They met weekly, after school, through the school year. The approach was unstructured, interaction moving wherever the needs and interests of the youth took it.

Quest-for-meaning groups: A west coast college set up small groups for all of its first year students, drawing on insights from our cultural heritage and using growth methods.

Youth-adult conversations: During the "nurture hour" on Sunday morning, a California church held a series of discussions involving some twenty youth and adults, co-led by a youth and an adult. The goal: "communication across the generation gap."

Youth retreats: A town in Arizona held an ecumenical youth retreat to "build bridges and deepen relationships." An intensive growth week or weekend on the trail, in a workcamp, or in an isolated spot can stimulate relating and reflection on life issues, and remotivate a dragging youth group.

Growth-oriented confirmation class: Departing from the usual didactic pattern, a church built its preparation-for-membership class around basic issues such as "Who am I?", "Who can I trust?", "Who is my brother?", "What is love?", "Who is God?", "What and where is the church?" Finger-painting, role-playing, trust and communication exercises were used to make the issues experiential. One of the sessions was a mini-marathon. None of the youth dropped out; all seemed "interested and committed." The leader reports that it was the most meaningful confirmation group in her experience.[6]

Action-reflection groups: Groups have proved to be invaluable during and after social action happenings—peace demonstrations, urban plunges, boycotts of economic exploiters, political campaigning—stimulating understanding of action skills and principles and new self-awareness. The experiences involved in community action should be used fully as personal growth opportunities.

The "Structured Growth Group":[7] The use of structure is sound in all youth growth experiences, but especially with junior highs. (With them frequent activity interspersed with brief times of verbal sharing seems to work best.) Role playing offers an excellent method of facilitating work on relationships in youth growth experiences. One high school group began a session by having each person finger-paint how he felt about life. The powerful feelings of conflict, loneliness, guilt, hope, passion, rage that came out "in living color," as one youth commented, opened the doors to honest, open sharing.

There are many other types of youth growth experiences which have proved to be productive. Bridging groups (cross-generational, interfaith, and intercultural) are important in our polarized society. To design groups that fit needs in your situation, convene a creative rap session of youth plus two open adults. In youth growth groups and particularly transgenerational groups, it is best to have a youth and an adult as co-leaders.

PREPARATION FOR MARRIAGE GROUPS

Every year the dreams of happiness of millions of couples end in nightmares. Premarital growth groups can prevent many of these painful tragedies by correcting their basic cause—lack of skill in relating, communicating, and nurturing a love relationship.

A religious center near the campus of an Iowa junior college offers "premarital growth and development groups."[8] The sign-up sheet announces that they are for "anyone thinking about getting married." The groups meet weekly, for six times (9:00 to 11:30 P.M.), led by a campus minister and his wife (married five years).

Chapters selected from *The Intimate Marriage*[9] are read by participants between sessions. Six couples have proved to be the optimal size. One recently married couple is included to stimulate discussion and share their experiences. Issues which come up frequently include "Not o.k. feelings," fighting, sex problems, hurting each other. A recurring comment among couples is— "You do that, too?"

Most "premarital counseling" is too short and surface-level to change the interpersonal ineptness and emotional deafness that foredooms millions of marriages to failure. Premarital sessions (usually one to three), with a clergyman or other professional, are much more likely to become actual counseling—i.e., go to the level of the couple's real needs—if they follow an engaged couples growth group. Courses on preparation for marriage and family life in schools usually do not reach the heart-and-gut levels where relationships are made or broken unless they include small growth groups.

The structure and process of premarital growth groups is similar to marital groups: a blending of *brief input* of relevant ideas (short films, for example); *skill practice* by couples (e.g., conflict-resolution methods); *awareness-communication exercises* in the total group; and plenty of *unstructured interaction* after each structured activity. *Home assignments* encourage couples to practice communicating on growth issues outside the group. Male-female co-leaders are best. Leaders should see each couple alone sometime during the group. The emphasis throughout should be on each couple's developing their resources for building together the relationship they want. Six to eight weeks, plus a marathon or retreat is a feasible format. Couples who need additional growth or counseling experiences, before or after their weddings, should be helped to find these.

Churches have a major role to play in providing premarital groups, since clergymen perform millions of weddings each year.

Groups should be scheduled and well-publicized at least three or four times a year. Interchurch groups are a possibility if individual churches do not have enough weddings to warrant even occasional groups. High schools, colleges, and community agencies should sponsor groups for both engaged and pre-engaged couples. High schools and churches must develop growth groups for fifteen to eighteen year olds, if the vast majority of youth are to be reached early enough to make a real difference. It is the intimate relationships that create or destroy human wholeness; therefore, providing a network of premarital growth groups is a high priority for our society. As every married person knows, to "be in love" is far from enough unless one also knows how to nurture that love so that it grows toward more satisfying, joyous intimacy.

TRAINING TO LEAD YOUTH GROUPS

Beyond the training described earlier, the issue for us adults who want to be youth group facilitators is how we *feel* about youth. This is determined largely by our relationship with one particular teen-ager—the one *inside us*. He's there, with our inner Child, whether we know him or not. If he's a stranger, he will distort our relationships with young people. He will cause us to fear them or "preach at" them. Keeping our Adult side (and not our Parent side) turned on in the presence of hostile or anxious adolescents will be almost impossible. So, to improve your effectiveness with youth, join a youth-adult growth encounter group to help you become a better friend to your own inner youth. Or, perhaps this fantasy will help:

Close your eyes and imagine a movie screen in your mind. Flash on it the house you lived in as an adolescent. Now picture yourself coming home from school. See yourself as you looked then. How do you feel? Picture some incident with your parents . . . with your closest friend . . . alone (feeling what you felt, in each case). Picture the most painful experience you can recall from those years. Feel it . . .

Recall the mess of feelings you had about sex . . . Make friends with the youth in your mind. . . . Chat with him . . . tell him how you feel relating to him . . . If he's still hurting, comfort him. You need each other very much.

When I use this reconnecting fantasy, I meet a lonely, pimply-faced lad at high school during lunch hour. He's wandering around alone because he's afraid to risk the rejection of his peers in the cafeteria. He's spending his lunch money at a corner grocery on milk and cake. The latter makes his pimples worse, but it's comfort of sorts for loneliness. Painful? Yes, but unless I keep connected with that lad and be a caring adult to him, his presence will foul up every effort to relate to youth. When I'm on good terms with him, this inner relationship is a bridge to other youth.

When you're in touch with your own youth of the past, encounters with youth and their culture become less threatening and more of a growth experience. It's important to listen to what they say and feel—after they trust you. It's difficult, particularly when their feelings about adult hyprocrisy "hits the fan." But, if you keep your Adult functioning you can gain new appreciation of the pain and the promise of youth.

THE GROWTH PERSPECTIVE AGAIN

"How come adults look at us as problems?" a youth group member asked. For a variety of reasons, our society conditions us to view young people as problems—a perception which they internalize in their self-image. Instead of thinking of themselves as *having* problems, which would simply make them a part of the human race, they tend to think of themselves as somehow *being* problems, which puts them in a special negatively important category. This fact underlines the importance of seeing young people through the growth perspective. If persons who matter see an individual affirmingly, in terms of his *being* and *becoming*, many of his problems diminish or even disappear. Few experiences do more to nurture self-esteem than encountering someone who sees us as valuable, both in who we are and in who we can become. Since what we can become is also what we deeply want to be, nothing is more likely to help us grow.

Additional Reading—Youth Growth Groups

("L" = of interest primarily to group leaders.)

L Blees, Robert A., and Staff of First Community Church, Columbus, Ohio, *Counseling with Teen-Agers*. Englewood Cliffs, N.J.: Prentice-Hall, Inc., 1965. See "Creative Use of Growth Groups," pp. 29-52.

Ginott Haim, *Between Parent and Teen Ager*. New York: The Macmillan Co., 1969.

L Jackson, Edgar N., *Group Counseling, Dynamic Possibilities of Small Groups*. Philadelphia: Pilgrim Press, 1969. "How Does the Group Method Work with Junior High Youth?" pp. 63-68. ". . . with Senior High Youth?" pp. 69-74.

L MacLennan, Beryce W., and Felsenfeld, Naomi, *Group Counseling and Psychotherapy with Adolescents*. New York: Columbia University Press, 1968.

L Ohlsen, Merle M., *Group Counseling*. New York: Holt, Rinehart and Winston, 1970. Chap. 10 "Counseling Adolescents in Groups."

Snyder, Ross, *Young People and Their Culture*. Nashville: Abingdon Press, 1969.

REFERENCES

1. I am indebted to Ralph H. Earle for this statement. Used with permission.

2. *Anne Frank, The Diary of a Young Girl*, translated from the Dutch by B. M. Mooyaart (New York: The Modern Library, 1952), p. 164.

3. Clarence A. Mahler, *Group Counseling in the Schools* (Boston: Houghton-Mifflin, 1969), p. 25.

4. Teen suicides increased by 100 percent in Los Angeles County in

1968-69. *Newsletter,* American Assn. of Orthopsychiatry, Vol. XV, No. 3, June, 1971, p. 6.

5. Abraham H. Maslow, "Self-Actualization and Beyond," *Challenge of Humanistic Psychology,* pp. 280-281.

6. Letter from Annette L. Aguilu, April 20, 1971.

7. For a description, see Robert A. Blees, *Counseling with Teen-Agers,* pp. 44-52.

8. Personal communication, Steve Marsh, May 31, 1971. Also Dorothy R. Freeman, "Counseling Engaged Couples in Small Groups," *Social Work,* October, 1965, pp. 36-42.

9. Howard J. and Charlotte H. Clinebell, *The Intimate Marriage* (New York: Harper & Row, 1970).

CHAPTER 7

Growth Groups for Children and Families

At each age and stage of their child's growth, parents experience themselves differently. They relive, often without realizing it, their comparable growth stage. . . . This reliving process can become a constructive thing, giving parents a second chance to do unfinished growth work. . . . This happens only if they are aware of what is happening and make the necessary effort. . . . A child's growth phases and struggles are really an invitation to continued growth on the part of his parents!

Crisis and Growth[1]

GROWTH GROUPS can be helpful in the difficult, challenging assignment faced by all parents. Parent growth groups offer indepth training in the art of parenting. Growth groups for children can facilitate a child's development by providing fulfilling experiences. Multiple-family groups can help whole-family units discover and develop their strengths. The goal of these family-oriented growth groups could be stated as "the self-actualizing person in the full functioning family."[2]

Parents face a king-sized challenge as the *primary growth enablers (or blockers) in their child's most rapid growth years.*

Almost all parents *want* to do a good job. Fortunately, most possess enough strength and love to succeed reasonably well. But parenting is getting more difficult; lightning-fast change increasingly widens the gulf between the worlds in which successive generations are formed. Somehow parents must help children learn broader, more flexible life-styles and role concepts which will be viable in the new world of tomorrow. To nurture healthier, more life-loving children capable of making something better of that unknown world—this is the need and the challenge. Growth groups can help. Every family, like every individual, has unused, or partially used, strengths, abilities, resources. A growth group aims at helping families mine this hidden gold.

GROWTH GROUPS FOR CHILDREN

The use of play therapy methods with "normal" children in nursery schools, elementary schools, Sunday schools, clubs, and homes can nurture growth and prevent many emotional problems from developing. Clark E. Moustakas, child therapist, describes these methods as "an opportunity to enter into a significant personal relationship with an adult in a situation where the boundaries are greatly expanded" and the child is free to express and play out usually forbidden feelings.[3]

A *play-growth group* for preschool or elementary school children should be small (three to six is best) and led by an adult who likes children, understands the basics of play therapy,[4] and isn't threatened by children's often violent feelings. Any warm, accepting, and emotionally stable parent or teacher can develop the skills needed for a play-growth group. The setting is a room where one doesn't have to worry about the floor and furnishings. Equipment may consist of paints and paper (both finger and brush types); families of dolls and puppets for fantasy play; clay for making and squashing things; a pan of water and a sand tray for messing; and lots of toys for encouraging release of pent-up aggressiveness—tanks, trucks, pounding boards, punching devices, and things for throwing or shooting without hurting. The adult's role is to encourage free expression, to be available to relate as the children reach out, and to enforce (if necessary) the ground rules—"Here we can do anything we like except hurt ourselves or others, or destroy property." Communication and expression by the children should be allowed to be spontaneous and free—through play, fantasy, words, paintings, acting with dolls, puppets, or whatever. Activities may be pursued individually or in spontaneous subgroupings of children. The facilitator doesn't pressure the children to discuss what they are doing, but he welcomes and encourages spontaneous communication.

A play-growth group encourages children to play out negative feelings (anger, jealousy, fear, guilt, destructiveness) so that these will not be expressed in self- or other-hurting behavior, nor block positive feelings (joy, love, pleasure, self-esteem), nor distort relationships. Play-growth groups provide opportunities to relate to other children in an atmosphere of openness and growth. They encourage children to use their imaginations in creative ways. Finally, they provide an experience of relating to an adult who values feelings, fantasy, and play—and can help each child use his unique inner resources in socially constructive ways. Such experiences allow a child to grow in his ability to relate and in his "it's-good-to-be-me" feelings.

Groups can help grammar school children deal with the big feelings related to the achievement of growth goals at that stage —feelings related to acquiring major language and mathematics skills, learning to function comfortably outside the home, and firming up relationships with the same-sexed parent and chums. Underuse of one's full potential in school (underachieving) often reflects fears and inner conflicts which can be resolved in a growth group. Although there is usually more verbal communication in such groups than in preschool groups, activities and play still predominate. The adult facilitator is available when the child is ready to discuss what he's doing and feeling. There may be brief sharing sessions as a group.

PARENT-LED GROWTH EXPERIENCES

Parents who are tuned to feelings can use home-grown play-therapy growth methods to help a child deal with crises such as the death or departure of a family member, an accident or natural disaster, a family uprooting, or a stress such as starting school. It can also be used at noncrisis times to free the child to employ and enjoy his strengths more fully.

Clark Moustakas recommends these principles:

(1) There should be a particular place to play. (2) A variety of play materials should be provided . . . [such as those described above]. (3) Children should be permitted to express what they wish and not be obliged to follow a model or product that meets a social or art standard. (4) No attempt should be made to interpret to the child the symbols involved in his play. . . . The child's own judgment and expressed feelings provide the best clues to the meaning of his play. They should be accepted exactly as they are expressed. (5) The parent should listen to the child's expressions, take his clues from the child, and convey full acceptance and understanding.[5]

There are excellent suggestions on parents' uses of play-therapy methods in several books about children.[6] A small play-growth group composed of one's own children, with perhaps several from the neighborhood, is one productive approach to using this method.

"Filial therapy" is a promising development in the mental health field. It involves training parents in groups of six to eight to conduct play-therapy sessions with their emotionally disturbed children in their homes. Parents continue to attend weekly group meetings with the trainer-therapist to discuss the play sessions and any other relevant matters. The children are not seen by the therapist. Instead, the parents, supported by the professional therapist and the group of parents involved in the same process, are responsible for the total therapy.[7] The possibilities of applying the filial therapy model to the growth work of normal children are exciting indeed. *A parents' growth group could be trained to use play-growth procedures at home concurrently with the life of the group.* Ideally, both parents should participate in the group and in leading the play sessions at home.

GROWTH GROUPS FOR PARENTS

Parent education does not automatically increase parental effectiveness. But it does to the extent that it helps parents *deal with their feelings* (including feelings about their children), increases their *head and heart understanding* of themselves and their children, and strengthens their *sense of competence* as parents. Churches, schools, and community agencies should provide such groups for parents of children at each family stage from prebirth through launching (adolescence). Each stage makes different demands; each offers new opportunities for family fulfillment. Parents can help the whole family become a growth group by learning to satisfy the psychological hungers of each other and their children. Changing male/female roles, which enable fathers to be more deeply involved in child nurture than ever before, increase the need for parent education beamed at them. The most effective parent growth groups are those in which mothers and dads are equally involved.

For the mental health of tomorrow's world, no groups could be more strategic than those for parents of infants and toddlers. In these crucial growth years, a child's basic foundation of trust or mistrust is developed. To be able to nurture a child's trust, parents must feel trust in themselves and each other. Parent growth groups for this stage should be *trust building groups*, attempting to reduce new-parent jitters, to give mutual support and an opportunity to share feelings, and to lessen the loneliness and anxieties connected with learning new parental roles.

A Long Island church sponsored a child-study nursery group meeting one morning a week throughout the school year. The group combined a child-study/growth experience for the mothers, child-care for infants, and a nursery school for preschoolers. A rotating steering committee was elected to plan programs and handle the mechanics of the meetings. An "interest finder" to identify needs was circulated periodically to all members as a basis of program-planning. The group was open to any mother of a preschool child in the church or community.

Sessions usually began with input to stimulate interaction: a film on children, a brief talk on a topic such as "developing confidence in children," a panel of mothers discussing an article on sex education for children, or some such activity. The interaction which followed often, though not always, reached a level of personal feelings, problems, and worries. Participants became a support-group to each other. As trust grew, the focus tended to broaden from childrearing to further discussion of their own needs. While the mothers met, a staff of six trained volunteers supervised the nursery school and provided baby care.

Evening meetings were held to share choice programs with husbands. In retrospect, it is clear that much greater involvement of the men would have increased the growth impact of the group. As it was, however, it met many needs.

Every stage of child development poses special stresses in parent-child relationships. Growth groups for parents of preteens and teen-agers can be highly productive. One church invited parents of the high school fellowship to a series of Sunday night discussion sessions using Haim Ginott's *Between Parent and Teen-Ager* as a stimulus for group interaction. A part of each evening was spent in a joint parent-youth rap session. The importance of intergenerational dialogue is increased by the urgent need to overcome the alienation from adults which many young people feel. Kingman Brewster, President of Yale University, has stated pointedly: "If the country does not rediscover its own sons and daughters, no amount of law and order or crisis management will make any difference in the long run."[8]

Parent Effectiveness Training[9] has demonstrated that many parents can improve relationships with their children through dynamic education in groups. Over fifteen thousand persons in two hundred communities have taken courses in this "school for parents." The program might be described as training and coaching in communication and relationship skills. (The same principles have now been applied in a Teacher Effectiveness Training program.)

An Oregon psychologist who has led P.E.T. groups reports that this approach attracts many people because it is explicitly *training* (not therapy) aimed at greater *effectiveness* (a positive, growth-oriented goal). It keeps the focus on relationships with one's children, not on relationships within the group. Active involvement and practice of essential skills are encouraged by role-playing and case illustrations.[10]

BEFRIENDING OUR INNER CHILD

In parent growth groups where the intent is to deal with whatever attitudes and feelings are distorting good parent-child relationships (as contrasted with the skill-training and discussion-type growth groups), it is be essential to help persons reconnect with their inner Child or Adolescent. One method for accomplishing this was described in the last chapter. In one group, each person was asked to draw a picture of himself as a child and then to reflect on it for a few minutes. Following this, he was asked to close his eyes, fantasy himself as a child at the age he had drawn, and then picture in his imagination some experience from his childhood, attempting to relive the original feelings. Subsequent discussion in the group revealed that several individuals had reconnected dramatically with their still active child feelings. The night after this experience, I had a powerful dream which gave me access to unresolved grief feelings from a painful loss early in my childhood.

Some ineffectiveness in parenting is rooted in unresolved guilt, dependency, and resentment toward one's own parents, living or dead. In growth groups, fantasy techniques may help resolve these feelings: "Picture yourself at the age when your feelings toward your parents were most intense . . . How do you feel? . . . Now, see yourself confronting your parents . . . tell them how you feel . . ." (At this point the person is invited to verbalize his feelings as intensely as he desires.) In one parents' group, a woman was able in this way to reduce her resentment toward rigid restrictions on her during adolescence. She discovered subsequently that this lessened the conflict with her teen-age daughter.

TRANSGENERATIONAL GROWTH EXPERIENCES

Parent/child and parent/teen relationships can often be enhanced by transgenerational group experiences. One such approach is play therapy with entire families participating.[11] Dad, mother, and children all come to the playroom. Each does what best expresses his own inner world and they interact with one another as they play and create. This approach has many possibilities for increasing well-family effectiveness in churches and community agencies, family camps and workshops.

One of many values of play—growth groups for adults is that they may reawaken the capacity to play—a capacity stomped down in many of us by long subservience to the work ethic. Spontaneous, expressive play—in contrast to the frantic "recreation" which is really a form of compulsive work—is itself liberating and growth-stimulating. It belongs in every growth group but it is particularly valuable as a bridge between generations in parent/child, parent/teen, and family groups. Children and youth watching adults play may be embarrassed (or amused) at first, but the experience may establish a positive bond linking the Child sides of each generation. Activities such as shared play therapy or a period of free movement to frolicking music in a group can awaken the spirit of playfulness.

The family growth conference or celebration is another transgenerational approach. In a session of one and a half hours with a growth-oriented counselor, pastor, or family-life educator, a family seeks to accomplish these goals: discover what each member appreciates and what he would like to change about the family; find out what each member thinks are the unused strengths of the family; get each person's suggestions for improving the family by using more of these strengths; set a few goals based on areas of agreement about improving things and using family strengths. (In the next session, progress toward these goals is reported.) After the checkup phase, growth in the family is celebrated with a party or something else the whole family enjoys. Families with good communication can conduct their own checkup/celebrations (perhaps with a rotating chairman). But an outside facilitator is essential in many situations, particularly for the first few sessions. Herbert Otto's *Family Strength Inquiry* is an action-oriented inventory which is useful in structuring the checkup around specific areas of family strength, thus avoiding the danger of getting sidetracked in a nongrowth, family pathology direction.[12]

FAMILY GROWTH NETWORKS

The health of a family is directly related to the strength of the supportive circle of relationships just outside the family. The biological clan (grandparents, aunts, uncles, within close range) no longer exists for most families. Therefore, to become true growth groups for their members, families need workable alternatives to the clan.[13] Fortunately, *functional families can become mutual growth facilitators to each other, by relating with continuity, openness, and caring!* The late Fred Stoller proposed a new structure which he called "the intimate network of families":

A circle of three or four families who meet together regularly and frequently, share in reciprocal fashion any of their intimate secrets, offer one another a variety of services and do not hesitate to influence one another in terms of values and attitudes.[14]

The idea emerged from experiences in *family workshops*—weekend growth meetings of three or four families aimed at developing more creative interaction. Openness and intimate sharing developed rapidly. A number continued to meet periodically after the workshops, developing at least a partially intimate network. Certain communes involving clusters of families are close approximations of family networks.

Growth-oriented family camps provide ideal settings for experiencing the people dynamic both within and among families. Camps which are designed for maximum growth provide small group opportunities for strengthening husband-wife, parent-child, whole-family, and family-to-family relationships. One such model included a daily *parents growth group, family cluster groups* (three families meeting together), and *marriage enrichment groups* (for couples, each evening). These were interspersed with opportunities for crafts, nature study, hikes, art, dramatics, dance, stories, games, as well as meals, rest, and a "family hour." One goal of this plan was to "help families form ties of friendship, caring and sharing, with other families—thereby developing a network of extended families."[15]

"Y" programs, in various places, have developed whole-family growth activities. For example, one YMCA in California sponsored a Saturday-Sunday Family Growth Workshop aimed at improving family communication. In Milwaukee, the "Y" sponsors Family Coteries, groups of eight to ten couples who are in the same stage of the family life cycle. A head couple is chosen by the group to work with the "Y" staff to discover program ideas which will meet the needs of these families. A monthly meeting of adults starts with a potluck meal followed by an educational or social program geared to the participants' needs. In addition, the families meet once a month for programs related to their interests. Once a year, the Family Coterie spends a weekend together to foster "in-depth relationships within and among the families." The goals of the Family Coterie program include: "developing communication between adults and youth, seeking a better understanding of ourselves . . . developing human relations skills, learning how to release the growth potential in the young, gaining a sense of balance in a world of confused values."[16]

Additional Reading—Family Growth Groups

("L" = of interest primarily to group leaders.)

Auerbach, A. B., *Parents Learn Through Discussion: Principles and Practices of Parent Group Education* New York: John Wiley, 1968.

L Axline, Virginia, *Play Therapy*. New York: Ballantine, rev. ed. 1969.

Axline, Virginia, *Dibs, In Search of Self*. New York: Ballantine, 1964.

Baruch, Dorothy W., *New Ways in Discipline*. New York: McGraw-Hill Book Company, 1949.

Clinebell, Charlotte H. and Howard J., Jr., *Crisis and Growth: Helping Your Troubled Child*. Philadelphia: Fortress Press, 1971.

Clinebell, Howard J., Jr. and Charlotte H., "Developing Parent-Child Intimacy," *The Intimate Marriage*. Chap. 8.

Ginott, Haim G., *Between Parent and Child*. New York: Avon Books, 1965.

Growth Groups for Children and Families
107

Gordon, Thomas, *Parent-Effectiveness Training*. New York: Peter
H. Wyden, 1970.

L Guerney, Bernard G., Jr., Ed., *Psychotherapeutic Agents. New
Roles for Nonprofessionals, Parents and Teachers*. New York:
Holt, Rinehart and Winston, 1969, Part 6.

Moustakas, Clark E., *Psychotherapy with Children, The Living
Relationship*. New York: Harper & Row, 1959. Chap. 8.

L Satir, Virginia, *Conjoint Family Therapy, A Guide to Theory and
Practice*. Palo Alto, Calif.: Science and Behavior Books, 1964.

REFERENCES

1. Charlotte H. and Howard J. Clinebell, Jr., *Crisis and Growth: Helping
Your Troubled Child*, pp. 32-33.

2. Ellis G. Olim, "The Self-Actualizing Person in the Fully Functioning
Family; A Humanistic Viewpoint," *The Family Coordinator*, July, 1968, pp.
141 ff.

3. Clark E. Moustakas, *Psychotherapy with Children*, p. 41.

4. See books by Axline and Moustakas.

5. Moustakas, *op. cit.*, p. 277.

6. See Chapter 8 in Moustakas; Guerney, Part 6; and Baruch, Part III.
Ginott's *Between Parent and Child* is a guide to the art of staying on the
child's wavelength.

7. Bernard, Guerney, Jr., "Filial Therapy: Description and Rationale,"
in Guerney, *Psychotherapeutic Agents*, p. 459.

8. Joseph Fletcher, "Generation Gap: Opportunity Lever," *The Churchman*, Aug/Sept., 1970, p. 6.

9. P.E.T. was developed in 1962 by Thomas Gordon.

10. Personal communication, Frank Strange, May 9, 1971.

11. Charlotte H. Clinebell has used this approach in her work as a child
and family therapist.

12. See Herbert A. Otto, "The Minister and Family Strengths," *Pastoral
Psychology*, April, 1966, pp. 21-28. The Pastoral Institute of Calgary now
has a "Marriage-Checkup" program for functional marriages.

13. The proliferation of communes in North America is in part a search
for a more supportive "family" by youth reared in isolated nuclear families.

14. "The Intimate Network of Families as a New Structure," *The Family
in Search of a Future*, p. 152.

15. Mrs. Edith Cole developed this plan for future use by her church
group.

16. From a brochure on "The Family Coterie," YMCA of Greater
Milwaukee.

CHAPTER 8

Growth Groups for Singles

Now the loneliness of the single parent is a strange thing . . . children . . . friends and relatives . . . and yet, over and over again, single parents speak of an "overwhelming recognition that I am alone," or of "realizing that I had to get on with it alone."

Parents Without Partners[1]

LIFE HAS more than enough frustration for all of us, but many who are divorced, widowed, or unmarried have even heavier loads. The more than 38 million single adults in the United States[2] live with loneliness, pressures and life experiences which are hard for most married persons to imagine. In these circumstances, growth groups can be particularly need-fulfilling.

If you're single—by choice or by circumstance—you probably have to work hard at building the need-satisfying relationships which all of us must have to survive. Here a growth group can be an asset. If divorce or desertion has left you single, a group is an investment in your future—a way to that difficult depth-learning which may help you avoid another marital booby trap. If the cruel hand of death has touched you, a group can help you cope with your loss. If you have the tough assignment of being a two-in-one parent to your children, a group of caring adults can be a sanity-saver. If the single state is what you prefer or have little chance of changing via matrimony, a group may help you establish other satisfying relationships. If your aim is to exchange your singleness for marriage, a group may increase the possibilities of developing a good relationship.

GROUPS FOR UNMARRIED YOUNG ADULTS

A young adult growth group was my introduction to the power of this method. Twenty-five years ago, my wife and I met weekly (from 6:00 to 7:30 A.M.!) with six to eight single young adults. Our goals were—to deepen our lives, strengthen our relationships and our faith, and discover ways to serve others more effectively. As a stimulus to sharing, we committed ourselves to certain reading and disciplines. Although I have learned much about small groups since that first exposure, I will always be grateful for the meaning that group generated for us as searching young adults.

Some unmarried young adults suffer from the freezing porcupines' dilemma*—they have intense needs for closeness yet cannot risk it because of fear of being hurt. Growth groups can provide emotional re-education[3] in how to get close to others so that one can discover that it's worth the risk. Achieving emotional/physical intimacy is the key growth task of young adults. Overcoming blocks to intimacy at this stage prevents the person from adopting distancing as a permanent life-style, and frees him to have deeply satisfying relationships (in or out of marriage). A group can help young adults increase those relationship skills which foster the intimacy essential to happiness for the single person or the married.

* Schopenhauer's fable describes two porcupines who alternately huddled together to avoid freezing and were repelled by the pain from each other's quills.

Patricia told her sharing group about her three unhappy engagements, each terminated by her. The group confronted her with questions about her pattern. At first she rejected Larry's comment that he "wondered if she would find a flaw in other candidates too." But, as she became aware of blocks in relating to men in the group, her broken engagements began to have new meaning. Eventually she could face and work on her fear of closeness to males—a fear that had become evident in the group.[4]

Growth groups are more than places to deal with hangups which otherwise diminish relationship enjoyment. Our culture ordinarily provides relatively shallow interaction between the sexes during dating and courtship (even if sexual intercourse is involved as it often is). The dating games that youth are programmed to play by our society, hide real needs, fears, and vulnerabilities. Growth groups encourage in-depth communication and allow persons to know each other without masks.

Many young adults, single and married, are searching for commitments that excite them. Groups can help such persons develop viable life directions that move beyond the necessary narcissism of youth to the generativity of adulthood. Finding the place where one's talents and the world's needs intersect isn't easy. But when it happens, tremendous growth occurs in both vocational and avocational areas. That first young adult group, mentioned above, aimed at becoming a cell of a more humane society. It expressed its intention in practical terms, by living frugally, contributing substantially (and encouraging others to contribute) to a fund for overseas relief.

GROWTH GROUPS FOR OLDER UNMARRIEDS

The marriage- and family-centeredness of our society creates an excluding climate for the unmarried. Furthermore, social prejudices and stereotypes toward older unmarried women make all their other problems in living more difficult. Deabsolutizing marriage and opening many socially valued options for women are objectives of Women's Liberation. As society moves toward these goals, growth groups can help free unmarried women (and men) to use their human potentials for enjoyment in living and fulfillment in relationships. Groups are particularly helpful in repairing the self-esteem damage of feeling a failure regardless of one's other accomplishments or a "reject" because one has not married.

Older unmarried men also encounter alienating social prejudices. One of these is the tacit assumption that they *must* necessarily have mother attachments or other neurotic problems, illustrating again that persons are not free to choose not to marry, without social stigma.

Sometime between thirty-five and forty-five, many single women confront the crisis that they probably will not marry.[5] Facing this crisis honestly and working through feelings about it, with the help of a group, can free a person to develop a more creative style of singlehood.

The growth perspective helps one to see the positive possibilities of being single. One of these is the opportunity to *use the enormous time and energy, which most couples invest in childrearing, in other forms of satisfying and socially useful creativity.* (Childless couples also have this opportunity of course.) Another is *the freedom and the motivation (need) to develop new models of relating.* There's no logical reason why one lifestyle—marriage—should be regarded as superior to every other. A single person can help develop a variety of other fulfilling options. A third positive thrust in singleness is *inescapable motivation to keep growing as a person.* Many married persons can avoid facing their emotional immaturity because it's protected by a neurotic marriage. This protection carries the high price of mutual stifling of personal growth. It's much harder for a single person to avoid the challenge to continue personal development.

A singles growth group can help one escape from the triple-trap of self-pity, self-rejection, and self-isolation. It can boost the "I'm o.k." feelings that liberate energy for using the positive potentials of singlehood. Just relating deeply to a small group of caring people increases feelings of interpersonal adequacy and cope-ability. It can help one establish familylike relationships to nurture continuing development. Such supportive relationships become increasingly important in overcoming the threat of loneliness in the mature years.

BEREAVEMENT RECOVERY GROUPS

Bereavement is the result of a psychological amputation. The wounded spirit heals gradually through an inner process called "grief work." In our death-denying society, normal grief work is often blocked and delayed. Beneath the surface, the wound remains unhealed. Frequently the unfinished grief produces destructive consequences. Counseling relationships often reveal that the onset of marital problems and of neurotic or psychosomatic symptoms followed a deep, largely-unresolved loss experience.

The raw, human suffering which could be alleviated by a network of support and sharing groups for bereaved persons is beyond imagination. Such groups offer encouragement to complete one's own grief work and to be a resource to others going through similar shadowed valleys. Growth groups have great potential for liberating grief-trapped people to say "Yes!" to life again.

Operation Second Life for young widows of men killed in Vietnam is a continuing growth group led by two psychiatrists at a Navy hospital in California. It meets two hours weekly with from six to ten members. None of the participants needs psychiatric help in the usual sense. Group membership is always changing as women recover from their grief and graduate after several months. One of the leaders describes the reality-therapy approach used:

The orientation of this group is viewed in the framework of health and normalcy (though) no attempt is made to curtail or suppress the normal mourning reaction. The major focus of the group meetings is on the "here and now" and on gaining an increased understanding of one's individual human potential. Although the past is not ignored, the emphasis is on helping each participant to better understand her own attributes and strengths.[6]

Discussion ranges widely—coping with children as both mother and father, decisions about where to live, feelings about the war, dealing with the reactions of in-laws, remarriage. One woman who hesitated to join the group, recalls: "At first I thought it would be very depressing with other widows, but I find it's very comfortable—comforting. There is an understanding (among us) that is almost like a bond." The psychiatrist believes it is this bond and the deep, supportive, and lasting friendships in the group which account, in part, for the rapid recovery from bereavement. He believes the program provides "an opportunity for a group of people sharing a common life tragedy to exchange constructive ideas, thoughts, and experiences which help them to deal with their lives in a more effective and satisfactory manner."[6]

In every community, groups for rebuilding life after major losses, sponsored by churches and counseling agencies, should be available. Leaders of such groups should keep in mind the two intertwined dimensions of recovery from loss:

1. The *feeling-catharsis aspect* involves experiencing and re-experiencing the pain of the loss and talking through the powerful feelings which otherwise may block the healing—guilt, resentment, self-pity, loss of meaning, anger, powerlessness, bitterness, deprivation, and fear. The leader, in this phase, encourages group members to talk about the lost person and his death. Experiencing the pain of this is part of the healing. If the leader suspects that guilt is infecting the grief wound, he may ask: "What would you do differently if you had a chance to live the relationship over

again?" Talking openly about one's guilt feelings in an accepting group takes the sting out of all except neurotic guilt.[7] Letting go internally of one's dependence on the lost person for satisfaction of heart-hungers is the difficult but essential transition to the second dimension of recovery.

2. The *re-entry-action aspect* of recovery involves rebuilding one's life minus the lost person and taking action to find new sources of need-fulfillment. After the first agonizing days, when the feeling task is central, there is a back and forth movement in the recovery process, between dealing with feelings and coping with the new demands of the reality situation. A growth group can help a person think through and evaluate the options open to him and then encourage him to begin taking small constructive steps. The action becomes part of the healing process—one feels better as one uses coping muscles to improve the external situation.

Persons who give no indication of recovering from their loss in a growth group may be suffering from a deeply infected grief wound. If so, getting the person to a skilled psychotherapist is essential.[8]

GROWTH GROUPS FOR DIVORCED PERSONS

Both death and divorce involve loss of spouse, sexual deprivation, change of status, and often economic problems. But, unlike the bereaved, the divorced person has few social guidelines to help him with his feelings and behavior; furthermore, he is more likely to experience judgmentalism from others and deep failure feelings in himself. Divorce, and the disintegrating relationship which led to it, often leave a grief wound infected by violent, conflicted feelings. Unless these are resolved and the wound heals, subsequent relationships will be distorted.

Some people move to greater maturity by using the pain of divorce as growth stimulus. Many, however, carry their problems

—which contributed to the demise of the first marriage—directly into subsequent relationships. Outside help (e.g., a counselor, or growth group) is usually essential if divorce is to be used as a significant growth opportunity. A well-functioning growth group can help one get a bead on one's problem-causing patterns and attitudes, facilitating change and thus preparing one for better relationships in the future.

A primary goal of post-divorce groups should be to enhance emotional maturity, the absence of which produces immense marital suffering. Berne's TA system is useful. According to this, emotional maturity is the degree of one's ability to keep the Adult side functioning in relationships; emotional immaturity is the degree of dominance of one's relationships by the Child side. The degree of emotional maturity can be recognized by the extent to which one *gives* love (rather than just taking it), tolerates frustration, possesses self-esteem, acts responsibly, respects differences in others, controls his impulses, perceives reality accurately, and empathizes with the feelings of others. Growth in these ways is the best preparation for remarriage (or any other close relationship).

SINGLE PARENTS GROWTH GROUPS

Charles Stewart tells of a retreat for fifty persons, all facing the problem of one-parent families:

Each one had a "story" which needed to be told but which, because of isolation, the hurry of work and care of children, or just plain lack of friends, had not been told to any emotional depth. As a totality they were "hungry for group life" and the retreat was set up to provide them with just that experience. . . . Each one, in small groups, talked in detail with other widows, widowers, and divorcees about their personal lives . . . they did not need encouragement to talk. They went at it the first night until past midnight, and I don't believe some slept at all the second night.[9]

Stewart found that they were concerned about the separation process involved in divorce or the death of a mate, the crises of rearing children alone, coping with the pervading sense of loneliness, handling the sex drive, and finding the powers of faith to overcome the "givens" of their situations.

Thirteen percent of U.S. families (one out of every seven and a half) have only one parent as a result of death, desertion, separation, divorce, or an unmarried parent. Growth groups can serve the needs of these parents:

By providing a support group to reduce loneliness, resolve grief, develop new relationship skills.

By giving substitute family ties for the children, thus reducing the heavy pressure of dependency on the single parent.

By letting the parent check out problems in childrearing, always complicated by the necessity to be a two-in-one parent, with an experienced and caring group of adults.

Parents Without Partners (and similar organizations) offers ongoing support groups in local communities. What is needed, in addition, are ad hoc groups with a specific growth orientation, sponsored by churches, schools, and community organizations, including PWP.

STARTING A MIXED GROUP

In a workshop for growth group leaders, the five single persons agreed to provide a "live" learning experience regarding growth groups for singles.[10] We sat in a small circle—two widows in their middle years, two young adult bachelors, a bachelor girl in her thirties, and myself as group facilitator—surrounded by the other workshop participants.

To become connected as a group, we put our hands in a stack in the center, closed our eyes, and experienced being together. Then we talked about how we felt—then and there, including our feelings about being observed. The outer circle was forgotten, for the most part, in the ensuing interaction. The recently bereaved woman shared her continuing struggles and grief. Several reached out to her with a touch. The other widow, resonating to the sharing by the first, spoke feelingfully about her marriage: "I still miss him terribly. I sing in the choir because I can't bear to sit alone in church."

The openness of feeling and risking took the whole group to a significant level. The unmarried woman (successful in her profession) described feelings of envy of the widows for their having been married and of the men for being able to take the initiative in relating to the other sex. The men shared experiences of "near misses," one having changed his mind only a few weeks before the wedding date. He expressed bafflement at why he had suddenly felt he had to withdraw just before moving into marriage on two occasions. He accepted the leader's invitation to see if he could get some light on what puzzled him. A significant clue may have emerged from this interchange:

Leader: What picture comes to your mind when you think of marriage?
Dwight: My parents' marriage—strictly all work and no play, rather dull.
Leader: It sounds as though marriage feels like a life of drudgery to you—almost like being sentenced to boredom.

After about thirty-five minutes of interaction, each person was invited to describe any directions of continuing growth which he had in mind. After this, the debriefing of the experience began. Even though it was a demonstration, real feelings were involved. Therefore, each person in the "growth group" was invited to discuss how he felt about the experience. Generally, the feelings (including the facilitator's) were of having had a much too brief, but genuinely meaningful, sharing—and a sadness that it was not feasible to continue as a group. I expressed my gratitude for their willingness to be open. We closed with a non-verbal group good-by and the discussion was opened to the other workshop members.

SEX AND THE SINGLE PERSON'S GROWTH

Conflicts and frustrations about sex are discussed frequently in singles groups which reach a level of honest sharing. Complicated enough for most of us, sex is a doubly difficult area for unmarried adults. For them, "abstinence and sublimation" are the only options which society and most churches have recognized as not "off limits" ethically. The majority ignore this advice,[11] but often at the price of guilt and inner conflict. Because of this, sex is often separated from relationships of trust, commitment, and caring.

In dealing with the issue of sex in a growth group, it's important to recognize that many of our culture's attitudes toward sex are contradictory and dehumanizing. The group should help individuals deal with their inner conflicts and rethink their personal values in terms of what constitutes person-enhancing sexuality for them. Many people (single and otherwise) hurt themselves and others by merely rebelling against old straight-jacket morality instead of struggling through to new values which are genuinely life-affirming.

Some basic changes are needed to humanize our mixed-up society which glamorizes sex on the one hand and officially denies it to 38 million adults on the other.[12] In the meantime, growth groups can help young adults who are striving to find ways to live constructively as human and sexual beings.

Churches and other organizations should sponsor both all-singles and mixed married-singles groups. As is true of any group in a common age category or life situation, singles groups offer an opportunity to concentrate on the special problems and challenges related to that situation and to learn from each other's experiences.

On the other hand, some single people prefer mixed groups and feel "segregated" if only singles groups are open to them. From the growth perspective, married and single persons are much more alike than they are different. The unifying concern of growth groups—developing one's fullest humanity—transcends the many differences which divide us. Homogeneous groups have an important function but so do mixed groups.

Additional Reading—Single Growth Groups

("L" = of interest primarily to GG leaders)

Egleson, Jim and Janet, *Parents Without Partners, A Guide for Divorced, Widowed, or Separated Parents.* New York: E. P. Dutton and Co., 1961.

L Goode, William J., *After Divorce.* Glencoe, Ill.: The Free Press, 1956.

Hugen, M. D., *The Church's Ministry to the Older Unmarried.* Grand Rapids: Wm. B. Eerdmans Pub. Co., 1958.

Jackson, Edgar, *Understanding Grief.* Nashville: Abingdon Press, 1956.

L Schlesinger, Benjamin, *The One-Parent Family.* Toronto: University of Toronto Press, 1969.

REFERENCES

1. Jim and Janet Egleson, *Parents Without Partners, A Guide for Divorced, Widowed, or Separated Parents,* p. 16.

2. The figure is higher now. In 1960, there were 21 million single women and 17 million single men.

3. If the fear of intimacy is intense, psychotherapy rather than a growth group is needed. Many older adults, married and single, suffer from the freezing porcupines' conflict.

4. Examples of young adult men with similar relationship problems could be cited. The "carefree bachelor" image is often a myth.

5. This crisis is discussed in an illuminating manner in Hugen's book, *The Church's Ministry to the Older Unmarried.*

6. Linda Mathews, "Viet Widows: A Side of War that Few See," *Los Angeles Times,* June 2, 1969, Part I, p. 3.

7. For a discussion of the distinction between neurotic and appropriate guilt see Clinebell, *Basic Types of Pastoral Counseling*, pp. 224-25.

8. See Jackson's *Understanding Grief*, Chaps. 11 and 12, for a discussion of pathological grief.

9. *Newsletter*, Institute for Advanced Pastoral Studies, November, 1965, p. 4.

10. This account provides a glimpse into the inner world of single people; it is presented with the permission of the group members.

11. Kinsey's studies showed that among single persons over 35, 87 percent of men and 48 percent of women had had intercourse at some time.

12. A task force of the United Presbyterian Church explored the issue of sex and single adults; it challenged the right of society to impose celibate standards on adults who do not choose them. Affirming marriage as the primary pattern of sexual relating does not preclude developing "a plurality of patterns which will make a better place for the unmarried." The report concluded: "Sexual expression with the goal of developing a caring relationship is an important aspect of personal existence and cannot be confined to the married and about-to-be married." *I.D.O.C.*, "Sexuality and the Human Community," January 30, 1971, p. 63.

CHAPTER 9

Growth Groups in Schools, Churches, and Agencies

What would happen if . . . the idea of developing human beings was considered so important and vital that each neighborhood had within walking distance a Family Growth Center which was *a center for learning about being human,* from birth to death? . . . human potential is infinite. We have only scratched the surface.

VIRGINIA SATIR[1]

THE FRAMEWORK and prototype of such a network of lifetime growth centers already exist—in the schools, churches*, and social agencies of our communities. But the vision of a more humanizing community can become a reality only as these institutions function more fully as *human growth and development centers!* These institutions hold the key to releasing the people dynamic in a community; they are the most realistic basis on which to create group growth opportunities for people of all ages.

ENLIVENING OUR INSTITUTIONS

Herbert Otto has pointed out that "The actualization of our human potentialities is closely bound to the regeneration of our human institutions. . . . We must begin with ourselves and

* Read "church and temple" whenever the word church appears.

the institutions with which we are most intimately concerned and connected."[2] Somehow we must continually revitalize the educational establishment, organized religion, and community agencies so that they respond to changing human needs— becoming (in John Gardner's words) "self-renewing institutions."

Growth groups can help in this renewal process. When leaders of institutions make groups a major thrust in both staff development and program, significant things happen. The level of participation and enthusiasm tend to rise as real human needs are met. In churches, the much-abused term "church renewal" becomes an experienced reality as congregations commit themselves to corporate ministries of mutual growth. People experience love, reconciliation, and grace in small communities of caring. The same enlivening occurs in schools where small-groups stimulate whole-person growth. In my own teaching, the discovery that growth groups and inductive methods of teaching theory can be combined in ways that strengthen both, has made a refreshing difference. In social agencies, growth-oriented groups are a practical means of moving to a prevention and fulfillment orientation and away from the repair-therapy orientation. Enhancing positive mental health in small groups for normal people may prevent many personal and family problems from developing.

An institution is vital to the extent that it is meeting human needs. In making decisions about types of growth groups to develop in any organization, listing unmet needs is the place to start. Which ages or groups within its constituency have the most pressing unmet growth needs? Among these, which hold the most promise of renewing the internal life of the organization to make it a more enlivening social environment? In schools, this question usually points to teachers and administrators. In churches, it points to clergymen and their spouses, lay leaders, and church school teachers. In agency settings, it points to administrators, counselors, and other staff members. Providing growth opportunities for these strategic groups is the most direct way to increase an institution's growth-stimulating vitality.

In all organizations, *potential small group leaders* are another high-priority target. Discovering natural growth facilitators and offering them a depth group experience is an efficient way of developing creative leadership for groups (growth and otherwise) within the organization. Several churches which now have a lively variety of growth groups did precisely this. They recruited the most emotionally mature persons available for the first group; those showing natural facilitator aptitudes were invited to obtain further training and then to co-lead groups with more experienced leaders. As more and more key people in any organization have growth experiences, the interpersonal climate and the program are gradually enlivened.

In his book *Joy, Expanding Human Awareness*, William Schutz declares:

Our institutions, our organizations, the "establishment"—even these we are learning to use for our own joy. Our institutions . . . can be used to enhance and support individual growth, can be re-examined and redesigned to achieve the fullest measure of human realization. All these things are coming. None are here, but they are closer. Closer than ever before.[3]

GROWTH GROUPS IN SCHOOLS

Schools can and should play a major role in providing growth opportunities for persons of all ages. Every community has its schools. If teachers, administrators, school boards, and parents catch a vision of schools as lifelong growth centers, the humanizing impact of this vast network of schools can be immense. In public and private schools, from prekindergarten through graduate and professional education, and continuing in a tremendously expanded adult learning program, growth groups can be used to release the people dynamic throughout society.

Good schools have always been growth centers. All genuine learning *is* growth. Skillful teachers are natural growth-facilitators. The growth group approach is a methodology for whole-person education by which teachers can increase their influence for growth. It is an approach which is effective in the most difficult and vital area of education—that involving feelings, attitudes, values, and relationships. These matters must receive increased attention if education is to equip people of all ages for full, responsible, joyful living. Norman Cousins describes humanizing education: "The first aim of education should not be to prepare young people for careers but to enable them to develop respect for life. Related lessons should be concerned with the reality of human sensitivity and the need to make it ever finer and more responsive; the naturalness of loving and the circumstances that enhance it or enfeeble it."[4] Growth groups offer a setting in which students and teachers can wrestle together with the value dilemmas and relationship problems which are central to the development of a workable life-style; they can promote the integration of relevant content from our culture in this process.

Teachers and administrators are keys to the growth climate of classrooms, faculty relationships, and administrative committees. Open, growing teachers tend to create growth-stimulating relationships with students. Administrators with firm and person–affirming styles tend to create growth-supporting schools. As suggested above, growth opportunities for these key persons are crucially important.

My wife and I have had a number of teachers in our growth groups. Often they were under heavy pressure in their jobs. They liked their work for the most part, but were "up to their ears" in discipline problems, staff tensions, criticisms from parents, and feelings of being sucked dry by the enormous needs of oversized classes. In some cases, the groups have helped them gain interpersonal satisfactions to offset job frustrations and have increased their communication and person-centered skills. A notable example was a fourth grade teacher who reported at the end of a group: "I've discovered here that it's o.k. to care and express it. What this has done to my teaching is amazing. The kids respond as if I were a different person!"

Peter Knoblock and Arnold Goldstein report on the use of group interaction to overcome professional loneliness and to further teacher growth. Six teachers met for seventeen sessions. Opportunity to talk out their ideas and feelings enhanced their ability to cope with daily classroom problems. They discovered a major untapped resource of experience and help—each other. Research findings on the group showed that the teachers had developed new listening skills, improved teacher-to-teacher relationships, and increased their understanding of themselves, each other, and their students.[5]

An Esalen program for teachers employs encounter, body movement, and sensory awareness techniques. Participants have developed innovative ways to integrate students' feelings, values, and relationships with the regular school curriculum.[6]

It behooves school administrators to make professional growth groups available to teachers who desire them as part of their continuing training. (It is also important for school boards and the community in general to understand the purpose of whatever small groups are used in a school system.) Since some teachers prefer to attend growth groups completely unrelated to the schools, community agencies have an opportunity to provide such groups. "Teacher Effectiveness Training" is one approach which has been productive with both professional (public and private school) and volunteer (church school) teachers.

Carl Rogers describes a plan for using encounter groups to awaken an entire school system from top to bottom. Beginning with a growth workshop for key administrators and board members, encounter groups are subsequently provided for interested teachers, students, and parents. Finally, a vertical group composed of two trustees, administrators, teachers, parents, excellent students, and failing or dropout students is held on the theme: "Our schools: What I like and don't like about them, and what I want them to be."[7] The emphasis is on developing a climate of openness and self-directed learning throughout the system.

Growth-group methods can be applied to classroom teaching to increase students' feelings of confidence and competence. William Glasser's open-ended classroom meetings, described in *Schools Without Failure*, are one illustration. In another educational innovation, the Human Development Program, children in groups of ten or so, for about twenty minutes each school day, participate in a variety of learning games. These allow them to experience success, deal with positive and negative feelings, discover something about relating, and learn that others have similar fears and concerns. Kindergarteners, for example, may receive and give fruit or candy to each other. Reactions to the exchanges are then explored by the children as they learn they have the ability to make others feel good. The goal of the program is to develop persons with healthy self-confidence as a foundation for maximum learning and for actualization of their potential.[8]

In addition to classroom growth methods, schools should develop a variety of other small groups for students, led by qualified teachers, counselors, and school psychologists. Two sources suggest the variety of growth group possibilities. Merle M. Ohlsen describes group counseling of adolescents and children in schools.[9] Helen Driver reports on two groups for high school seniors, three groups for college students, and four leaderless teachers' groups.[10] The second part of Driver's book reports on forty-four projects using small groups in elementary, high school, college, and graduate professional schools (as well as mental health settings), as described by the leaders of each group.

Growth groups are being used increasingly with college

students in ecumenical student religious centers, in psychology and human relations courses, in training of dorm counselors, and in college guidance programs. Three psychologists who use growth groups at the University of California at Davis state: "This small group approach, bringing persons together in an atmosphere of community and trust, fairly explodes with antidotes for what ails higher education. . . . The basic mode of the encounter group is relevance, the actual, the real, and the here-and-now. . . . The encounter process stresses openness, transparency, and clear and effective communication. . . . It helps to reduce the barriers of roles and styles of living which keep apart and prevent understanding."[11]

Since the professional effectiveness of teachers, ministers, social workers, counseling psychologists, nurses, and psychiatrists depend so much on their skills in relating and communicating, graduate schools training them should make extensive use of growth groups. My experience with professional growth groups for theological students over the last decade has convinced me that the quality of professional services could be raised significantly in a few years if growth groups were used widely in professional education. It takes more interpersonal competence to be effective in any of the person-centered professions today than it did in a less chaotic time. Groups offer opportunities to integrate the knowledge of one's profession with essential interpersonal skills in the formation of one's professional identity.

Relationship training will undoubtedly be increasingly emphasized in adult education. Junior and senior colleges, university extension departments, churches, high schools, and community agencies should provide high-quality groups with an emphasis on learning to love, to create, to enjoy, to relate, to communicate. As leisure increases, both the need and the possibility for such in-depth learning groups will also increase. George Leonard puts the challenge well: "Education in a new and greatly broadened sense can become a lifelong pursuit for everyone. To go on learning, to go on sharing that learning with others may well be considered a purpose worthy of mankind's ever-expanding capacities"[12] Education, in this perspective, becomes not a time-limited preparation-for-living but an ongoing way of life. Small groups can help to nurture this lifelong growth. Their goal is to make learning "as relevant, involving, and joyful as the learning each of us experienced when we were infants first discovering ourselves and our surroundings."[13]

GROWTH GROUPS IN CHURCHES

Churches should play a strategic part in the growth network needed to develop the unused human potentialities in every community. No other institution in American life has regular, face-to-face contacts with so many millions of adults. The small group approach is a natural in the church, undergirded by a long tradition. The right of each person to develop his full potential as a child of God is basic in the Jewish-Christian heritage. Many church leaders—clergy and laity—are discovering the power of groups for implementing this right. Robert Leslie, a pioneer in using small groups in the church, now reports: "An increasing number of people are finding new meaning in their church life through small sharing groups. More and more ministers are finding a new focus for their ministry in developing group life."[14] Relevant churches have a three-pronged mission: to *heal* brokenness, to *nurture* growth, and to *equip* (train, coach, educate, inspire) change/growth agents to help individuals and to create a more humanizing society. Growth groups are useful in each of these thrusts.

I concur with George Webber's conviction that a congregation in mission "will make basic provision for its members to meet in small groups (as well as corporate worship), not as a sidelight or option for those who like it, but as a normative part of its life."[15] A viable motif for the church in the last third of the century is found in words attributed to Jesus in John's Gospel: "I have come that men may have life . . . in all its fullness" (John 10:10, NEB). To implement this motif in mission, a church must become a human wholeness and training center.

Churches have several unique advantages and resources which can be utilized in growth groups. Since all eight life stages are represented in a congregation, there's a splendid opportunity to *develop a full ladder of growth groups.* Small groups can help people prepare for normal, developmental crises (e.g., adolescence) and cope with unexpected, accidental crises. The vertical orientation of the church fellowship defines another unique resource—*an explicit concern for nurturing spiritual growth* by helping people develop functional adult values and philosophies of life and thereby strengthen their connection with the Source of life and growth. Spiritual growth involves deepening one's sense of "at-homeness" in the universe and increasing one's awareness that "I'm O.K.—You're O.K.—God's O.K." God is very dead for many people. The concept refers to no reality in their actual experience. God can be revived for them only in relationships where theological truths become experiential realities. This can happen in growth groups. At the close of two weeks of daily growth group sessions, participants in one workshop could identify these biblical themes in their shared experiences: bondage and liberation, salvation by grace, judgment, death and rebirth, alienation and reconciliation, mutual caring, the transforming power of love, becoming a spiritual unity, growth.

Church groups can contribute to spiritual growth by utilizing basic insights from their heritage. This heritage holds that man is more than "a larger white rat or a slower computer"[16]—his freedom, awareness, valuing, caring, and creativeness constitute the core of his humanness. These spiritual aspects (called the "image of God" in traditional language) are what make man human. Growth in these increases his humanity. From the religious perspective, human potentializing is not so simple as an acorn becoming an oak. Man takes part in creating or distorting his own future; he is to a degree self-determining.

The human potentials movement needs the emphasis of the Hebrew-Christian tradition (and of Freud) on man's powerful tendencies to resist, block, and distort the growth drive. Simplistic growth models such as unfolding flowers are deceptively attractive but inadequate when applied to the complexities of human life. The recognition that "dying" precedes rebirth is a valuable part of ancient Christian wisdom (expressed symbolically by crucifixion preceding resurrection). In groups this truth becomes experiential as the painful dying of life-constricting defenses and patterns of relating precedes rebirth to more intimate, vital relationships. From their heritage, church groups should be aware that ultimately all growth is a gift and a mystery. Grace, the love we do not have to earn, is the power that produces growth. Forgetting this, infatuation with our techniques can make them sterile and manipulative. A sense of the ultimate mystery of all life and all relationships should remind church groups that there are no psychological answers to the deepest dimensions of any human problems. For the normal anxiety and existential loneliness which are inescapable parts of man's self-awareness, only spiritual and philosophical answers satisfy.[17] To help persons find these is that part of a growth group's task to which a church group brings unique resources.

In developing church growth groups, it helps keep their unique perspectives and resources accessible if their purpose is described theologically as well as psychologically. A church's group plan should have two parallel thrusts—(1) *developing groups with explicit goals of personal/marital/family growth*, and (2) *infusing regular, ongoing church groups with a stronger growth emphasis*. In larger churches, the eventual aim of the first thrust should be to make a variety of growth experiences available to all interested persons at each stage and interest category. In smaller churches, a leaders' group, one for couples, one for youth, and one mixed group are usually feasible.

Priority should be given to establishing certain types of groups: As indicated earlier, one of these is *a group for church officials, other lay leaders, teachers,* and *youth leaders.* Reaching these persons is the most efficient way to infuse ongoing groups with a growth emphasis. *Marriage enrichment groups,* particularly for new and expecting parents, should have priority. As the only institutions with direct entreé to millions of new families, churches have a strategic responsibility to provide growth experiences for those who have or will soon have awesome influence over the mental health of small children.

Since spiritual growth is an explicit concern, special *spiritual enrichment groups* should be developed in churches. (Spiritual development should be emphasized in all groups as part of whole-person growth.) Depth Bible study groups, Yokefellow, and Koinonia[18] groups are approaches which combine deepening one's faith and relationships. *Crisis support groups* should be available as part of a church's growth opportunities. When crises are handled well, they produce growth. A middle-aged widow told how an informal support group (of former church school teachers) rallied round when they received word that her teen-age daughter had run away. "I believe I would have come unglued without that group!" she stated. *Bereavement recovery groups,* as suggested earlier, should be available in every church. As the only professionals regularly involved with the family after death occurs, clergymen have *the* major responsibility for facilitating recovery from grief. By helping persons complete their "grief work," small groups can liberate potentialities for fuller living. In many churches, those in crises, including bereavement, may become a part of mixed growth groups.

Action-Growth groups can express both the pastoral and the prophetic ministry, and should have priority in a church's group program.

After several months in a Bible study-growth group (led by their pastor) the members began to look for ways to share their new awareness of relationships and the Christian life in their community. They decided to do something about the white suburban ghetto in which they lived. First they invited persons from the half-dozen black families in their community, to join the group. Several accepted. Over the next few months they had the experience of relating in depth across racial lines, around biblical issues. Then they decided to spearhead efforts to get open housing in their community. Drawing in allies from other churches and community groups, they formed an open housing task force which is engaging in a continuing effort to implement the ideals of religion and democracy in housing practices.[19]

Caring teams of laymen can best be trained in growth-action groups. Warm, confident, and accepting people are chosen and trained to work as volunteers, under the minister's direction, calling on shut-ins, the sick, newcomers, and the bereaved. After trying several approaches, I now believe there are three ingredients in effective training: (1) Brief *input sessions* presenting, with abundant illustrations, simple, operational tools such as reality therapy and crisis-helping methods. (2) *Skill practice and supervision*—for example, role-playing a call on a bereaved person. (3) *Personal growth experiences in a small group* where the integration of ideas and skills can occur. The group's trainer-facilitator should keep a balance between personal growth and training for helping others. This kind of relationship training should be available to all church groups which do lay calling for budget raising, membership recruitment, parish shepherding, etc., to increase their interpersonal skills.

In addition to these high-priority groups, churches should develop other growth opportunities, guided by the need-pattern of particular congregations and communities.

The pastor of a Massachusetts congregation decided to do something about the superficial relationships which make many churches "communities of strangers." Attempts to recruit separate growth groups were unsuccessful because of crowded schedules. The alternative was to introduce a growth emphasis into regular boards, committees, and meetings. By streamlining business, time became available for deeper sharing. In approaching each group, the minister explained his intent and asked permission to introduce certain experiences of relating. Several women's groups turned from primary concern with the institutional church to community projects, as a result of the "new flavor" developed in the groups through interpersonal deepening.[20] It has been my experience that many larger church meetings, including worship services, can be enlivened by incorporating small group communication and awareness experiences into the proceedings.

Growth groups *can* be effective in small churches and in small communities. The minister of such a church, who has developed two groups, reports that small-town anxiety about secret-breaking sometimes deters deep sharing. But assets outweigh liabilities. The groups have bridged differences between several people, opened individual counseling opportunities, let parishioners express "beefs" directly, and given the minister support in his ministry.[21] I concur with Robert Leslie's suggestion that the most natural, unthreatening way to introduce personal sharing in churches is to combine this emphasis with study. This is essential in many rural and conservative areas where resistance to newer group approaches exists.

Larger churches can develop a variety of growth groups. An Oregon church uses its groups to serve both its members and its community. One of the ministers describes the church groups:

The congregation has five growth groups (called Interpersonal Support Groups) in which various growth skills are taught and practiced. There are also five fellowship groups, without a growth agenda, but with some growth results. There is a great correlation between those who are group participants and those who have leadership in the congregation. . . . The congregation is unusually candid about expressing what they think and openly expressive of warmth. In short, there are more freed people around. . . . We continually educate the older members about the nature of these programs. This is necessary in order to have staff time allowed for them.[22]

The church also has student-adult communication groups, Yoke-fellow groups, and Functional Department Groups (combining growth and task objectives).

This church reaches out to the needs of its community by sponsoring and staffing two sessions of Parent Effectiveness Training and one of Teacher Effectiveness Training each year. Recently the church has begun weekend Marriage Effectiveness Training groups. Approximately 90 percent of participants in these three programs are not members of the sponsoring church.[*]

The impact on a church of its growth groups is evident in this report from a minister in California:

Small growth groups have added a real flavor to the life of our congregation. . . . they are the persons who are most involved in the life of the church at all levels. They have made our church a community in their reaching out to others out of their own self-fulfillment. I personally have benefited from these groups. I am constantly affirmed in seeing persons change, but even more so by their love and appreciation for me and my skills in group work.[23]

Clergymen have exciting, demanding jobs as growth facilitators in churches seen as human-development centers. Their commitment is to liberate, enlarge, deepen, and enrich the pro-life

[*] A number of churches in various parts of the country have sponsored or cooperated in growth centers which serve their communities by offering growth workshops, institutes, and retreats.

forces in families, individuals, and social institutions—and to equip laymen for their enlivening work in the congregation and community. To be effective as an enlivener of others, a clergyman should have his own growth group for continuing professional renewal. The minister and his wife should be in an ongoing marriage growth-support group in order to nurture their own relationship. The strange new world we live in opens unprecedented opportunities for ministries to persons. But it also demands more resourcefulness, more spiritual guts, more love with muscles. To meet this challenge—to minister to the new age—a clergyman must acquire new tools; more important, he must be open to becoming a new person—more aware, caring, and alive. That is why he needs a growth group on a continuing basis.

GROWTH GROUPS IN COMMUNITY AGENCIES

If growth groups are to become maximally available and effective, community agencies must play a major role. Many persons who are not likely to join groups in churches and schools may do so if they're made available in family counseling agencies, mental health services, youth organizations, business and industry, fraternal groups, self-help groups (such as A.A., P.W.P., Alanon, etc.), and in the many organizations devoted to special needs—of the handicapped, ex-prisoners, ex-patients, unwed parents, minority groups of all kinds, senior citizens, community action groups, ethnic organizations. Furthermore, the effectiveness of many agencies and organizations can be increased significantly by utilizing growth groups to achieve their particular goals-for-people.

Growth groups have a role in both the preventive and treatment aspects of *community mental health services*. Growth groups should have a central place in the after-care programs which follow intensive treatment. Community networks of groups for families of patients and ex-patients would improve the interpersonal environment which supports or sabotages full recovery of the patient. In a survey of the ways groups are used in mental health centers, psychiatrist E. Mansell Pattison found that one of the most frequent uses is in *consultation services* for those in the care-giving professions.[24] In the Los Angeles area, for several years, small groups of clergymen met with consultants supplied by the community mental health centers to discuss counseling relationships in their parishes. These groups had a double value—they were an efficient use of the consultants' time, and, as mutual learning and support occurred, they became professional growth groups for the ministers.

Mental health education is most successful in growth groups where the principles of mental hygiene can be applied in personal ways, ways which take into account the feelings, attitudes, self-image, and relationships of those involved. Groups also have a major role in *training mental health personnel*—professionals, paraprofessionals, and nonprofessional volunteers. Pattison's survey revealed that a surprising 41 percent of the centers provided some type of personal growth group for their professional trainees. The training of the nonprofessionals who staff the effective Marriage Guidance Centers in Australia and elsewhere is done mainly in groups.

Mental health centers should also offer growth-oriented groups to clients. A surgeon on a medical school faculty came to a private mental health clinic with this question: "At forty-two, I'm a high-level technician. Where can I go to learn how to live?" An innovative psychologist responded to this challenge by setting up a growth group called a "School for Living," aimed at actualization of potentialities and increasing effectiveness in living.[25] This approach is now being used in a state rehabilitation of the handicapped program.

Many family, marriage, and child counseling agencies make use of growth groups, particularly in family life education programs. The Pastoral Institute of Calgary has an extensive program of

small group education for family living. The director of this program describes why they prefer to use the growth group approach: "It is in the dynamics of a small group that we experience
the interactions, feeling responses, and behavior patterns of our
own family's relationships—and others. A small group provides
a catalytic learning situation with . . . emotional involvement
and safety, under the guidance of a leader-facilitator, in which
intellectual, feeling and behavior learning can best take place."[26]

Many of the 340 Family Service Association of America agencies use growth groups in their family life education. A counselor
in one such program comments on the values of this approach:
"Individual concerns and frustrations are handled, feelings are
recognized and shared. The participants try new methods, then
bring up the same topic in other meetings. Some topics such as
sex education, handling of anger . . . may be main topics for
three or four sessions."[27]

The "Y" is using growth groups for both staff training and
service to youth and families. The National Board of YMCA's
sponsors a Family Communication Skills Center to help "Y's"
develop programs for families. Local "Y's" use Parent and Teacher
Effectiveness Training and family crisis prevention groups in
workshops for training staff and lay group leaders.

Business and industry have made extensive use of growth
groups to improve human relations within their organizations.
"Organizational Development" (O.D.) is an approach which
attempts to "integrate individual needs for growth and development with organizational goals and objectives in order to make
a more effective organization."[28] It has been used by school systems, religious organizations, governmental agencies, as well as
business and industry. The goal of O.D. can be described by
Abraham Maslow's term "synergy"—the state which exists when
an organization is so arranged that an individual in meeting his
own needs also meets the needs of others and the organization.[29]

O.D. is an illustration of how growth group principles can, by taking human relationships and needs seriously, be used to accomplish tasks more effectively.

GROUPS THROUGH THE LIFE CYCLE

To maximize the fulfillment of human potentials, the organizations of a community—schools, churches, agencies, and others—should develop small groups designed to meet the growth needs of persons at each of the eight life stages. An overview of these stages and some groups which are relevant to each may suggest new possibilities for groups which can be developed in your organization. The following chart lists the stages as delineated by Erik Erikson;[30] some groups which can help accomplish the growth goal of each stage (column 2); and some groups to meet the needs of "significant others" at each stage (column 3):

Stage and Life Task	Growth Groups for Persons in this Stage	Growth Groups for Significant Others
Stage 1: IN-FANCY (Birth to 15 months) *Life task:* Developing BASIC TRUST, through a loving, dependable, nurturing relationship with parenting persons. *Key question*: Can I trust my world, myself?		Expectant parents growth groups. Parents growth groups for support, learning, catharsis, trust-strengthening. New Parents marriage growth groups for couples. Groups for adults involved in nurseries, babysitters. New Grandparents growth group. Prebaptismal training groups.

Stage and Life Task	Growth Groups for Persons in this Stage	Growth Groups for Significant Others
Stage 2: EARLY CHILD- HOOD (15 months to 2½ years)	Nursery groups. Toddlers creative play groups.	Parents support, sharing, and fellowship groups to meet the needs of this stage—their own and their child's. (Each stage 1–5.)
Life task: Developing a sense of AUTONOMY while retaining basic trust.		Parents growth group combined with nursery for child. Ongoing training group for nursery school workers (church & nonchurch).
Key question: Can I be an individual and not lose the love I also need?		Group for parents of handicapped children —(all stages).
Stage 3: PLAY AGE (2½ to 6 years)	Pre-school nursery groups. "Play therapy" adapted to stimulate growth of nondisturbed. "Head start" group for children from culturally impoverished back- grounds.	Parents growth groups to meet the needs of this stage—theirs and their child's. Family growth nights, weekends, camps.
Life task: Developing a sense of INI- TIATIVE.		Child and family crea- tivity groups—dance, art, music, drama, myth-creating, etc.
Key question: Can I prize and exercise my growing sense of strength and thrust?		Single-parent groups (at each of first 5 stages).

Stage and Life Task	Growth Groups for Persons in this Stage	Growth Groups for Significant Others
Stage 4: SCHOOL AGE (6 to 12 years)	Clubs and activity groups for boys or for girls. Junior and junior high camps, and conferences. Discovery groups—emphasis on creative activities, play that develops skills and competencies. Confirmation-growth classes. Play therapy groups for the non-disturbed. Relationship, sex, and drug education groups. Tutoring groups, using older students.	Parents growth groups, to help them begin to release the child. Leader and teacher growth groups for adults leading groups at this stage. Parent-child groups: father/son; mother/daughter. Family nights: fun, study, worship, sharing. Family checkups. Family camps. Child-family creativity groups.
Life task: Developing a sense of INDUSTRY, and of one's role as a boy or girl. *Key question:* Can I acquire competency in the basic skills of my culture?		
Stage 5: ADOLESCENCE (Puberty to 20)	Teen discovery groups: Boy/Girl relations, getting along with parents, decisions about drugs, alcohol, sex, vocational choices. Identity search groups. Work/worship/play groups. Premarital growth groups. Depth study groups. Retreats, camps, trail hikes, task groups, social action groups. Coffeehouse groups; drop-in center; rap sessions. Self-other awareness groups.	Parent study and growth groups. (See Middle years.) Parent support groups to cope with stresses of adolescents in home. Parents group to work on their own unfinished identity and conflicts stirred up by teens. Joint parents-youth groups—series, camps, retreats; generation-gap bridging groups.
Life task: Developing a strong sense of IDENTITY. *Key questions:* Who am I? As a male or female? What is my worth? What are my own values?		

Stage and Life Task	Growth Groups for Persons in this Stage	Growth Groups for Significant Others
	Preparation for marriage groups. Preparation for parenthood, college, leaving home, etc. "Search for meaning" groups. Ecology growth groups.	
Stage 6: YOUNG ADULT- HOOD	Single young adult growth group: "Deepening Relationships." Preparation for marriage group. Newlyweds growth group: Building your marriage. (Groups for young parents —see Stages 1, 2 and 3). Family network groups: several young families. Marriage Liberation groups. "Alternatives to Marriage" groups.	(See groups for children in stages 1–4.)
Life task: Developing INTIMACY		
Key questions: Can I establish close and meaningful relationships?		
Stage 7: MIDDLE ADULT- HOOD	Mid-Years Marriage Enrichment group. Generativity groups: evaluating oneself investment plan (philosophy of life). Growth through service groups: personal caring teams; social action task groups. Depth study groups: with a personal growth focus.	(See groups for adolescents and young adults, stages 5 and 6.)
Life task: GENER- ATIVITY (generating life through investing oneself in society)		

Stage and Life Task	*Growth Groups for Persons in this Stage*	*Growth Groups for Significant Others*
Key question: Can I find my fulfillment through giving to the ongoing stream of life?	Spiritual search groups. Discover-Your-Hidden-Talent group. Your Second Vocation group. Preparation for Constructive Retirement group. Groups for parents of teens (see Stage 5) and emptying nest.	
Stage 8: OLDER ADULTHOOD Life task: Developing "EGO INTEGRITY," by accepting and affirming one's life. *Key question:* Can I make peace with my finitude, accept my brief place in life with gratitude and serenity? Can I experience and prize those things which transcend my finitude?	Creative activity groups: depth study groups; art groups; contemporary issues groups; prayer and share groups. Service groups aimed at the needs of older adults and others in the community; dual focus on service and personal growth; group to use the many rich talents of retired persons. Spiritual growth groups. Bereavement group for working through losses of various kinds. Grandparent and foster-grandparent groups. Constructive retirement groups. Social action group. Transgenerational group.	Groups for young and mid-adults whose parents are now leaning on them.

Growth groups provide opportunities to discover ways of satisfying one's personality needs in the changing relationships, demands, frustrations, and possibilities of each new stage. As a strategy for helping persons cope constructively with the normal crises of human development, they are without equal. The most effective way to make your organization a human development center is to create growth groups to meet the needs of your members at their varying life stages.

Additional Reading

FOR TEACHERS AND SCHOOL GROUP LEADERS:

Borton, Terry, *Reach, Touch, and Teach: Student Concerns and Process Education.* New York: McGraw-Hill, 1970.

Cantor, Nathaniel, *The Teaching-Learning Process.* New York: The Dryden Press, 1953.

Driver, Helen I., *Counseling and Learning through Small-Group Discussion.* Madison, Wis.: Monona Publications, 1958.

Glasser, William, *Schools Without Failure.* New York: Harper & Row, 1969.

Guerney, Bernard G., Jr. (Ed.), "Teachers as Psychotherapeutic Agents," *Psychotherapeutic Agents,* pp. 337-380.

Holt, John, *How Children Learn.* New York: Pitman Publishing Co., 1967.

Leonard, George B., *Education and Ecstasy.* New York: Delacorte Press, 1968.

Mahler, Clarence A., *Group Counseling in the Schools.* Boston: Houghton Mifflin, 1969.

Morris, S. B., *et al.,* "Encounter in Higher Education," in Burton, *Encounter.* San Francisco: Jossey-Bass, 1970, pp. 189-201.

Ohlsen, Merle M., *Group Counseling.* New York: Holt, Rinehart and Winston, 1970.

Rogers, Carl R., *Freedom to Learn.* Columbus, Ohio: Charles E. Merrill, 1969.

Sharp, Billy B., *Learning: The Rhythm of Risk.* Rosemont, Ill.: Combined Motivation Education Systems, 1971.

FOR CHURCH LEADERS:

Anderson, Philip A., *Church Meetings that Matter*. Philadelphia: United Church Press, 1965.

Casteel, John L. (Ed.), *The Creative Role of Interpersonal Groups in the Church Today*. New York: Association Press, 1968.

Clinebell, Howard J., Jr., "Group Pastoral Counseling," *Basic Types of Pastoral Counseling*. Nashville: Abingdon Press, 1966, Chap. 12.

Clinebell, Howard J., Jr., "Mental Health and the Group Life of the Church," *Mental Health through Christian Community*. Nashville: Abingdon Press, 1965, Chap. 7.

Leslie, Robert C., *Sharing Groups in the Church*. Nashville: Abingdon Press, 1971.

Reid, Clyde, *Groups Alive—Church Alive, The Effective Use of Small Groups in the Local Church*. New York: Harper & Row, 1969.

FOR AGENCY GROUP LEADERS:

Argyris, Chris, *Integrating the Individual and the Organization*. New York: John Wiley and Sons, 1969.

Gifford, C. G., "Sensitivity Training and Social Work," *Social Work*, Vol. 13, No. 2, April, 1968, pp. 78-86.

Golembiewski, R. T., and Blumberg, Arthur (Eds.), "Where Can T-Group Dynamics Be Used?: Applications in the Home, School, Office, and Community," *Sensitivity Training and the Laboratory Approach*. Itasca, Ill.: F. E. Peacock, 1970, pp. 289 ff.

Maslow, Abraham, *Eupsychian Management*. Homewood Ill.,: Richard Irwin and The Dorsey Press, 1965.

Scheidlinger, Saul, "Therapeutic Group Approaches in Community Mental Health," *Social Work*, Vol. 13, No. 2, April, 1968, pp. 87-95.

Schutz, William C., "Task Group Therapy," *Joy, Expanding Human Awareness*, pp. 209-213.

Schwartz, William, and Zalba, Serapio, R. (Eds.), *The Practice of Group Work*. New York: Columbia University Press, 1971.

REFERENCES

1. Virginia Satir, "Marriage as a Human-Actualizing Contract," *The Family in Search of a Future*, New York: Appleton, 1970, p. 59.

2. Herbert Otto, "The New Marriage," *The Family in Search of a Future*, New York: Appleton, 1970, p. 112.

3. New York: Grove Press, 1967, p. 223.

4. Norman Cousins, "See Everything, Do Everything, Feel Nothing," *Saturday Review,* January 23, 1971, p. 31.

5. Peter Knobloch and Arnold Goldstein. *The Lonely Teacher.* Boston: Allyn and Bacon, 1971.

6. George B. Leonard, *Education and Ecstasy,* p. 220.

7. Carl R. Rogers, *Freedom to Learn,* pp. 303-323.

8. "Magic Circles in the Classroom" (abstracted from an article by Harold Bessell), in *Sensitivity Training and the Laboratory Approach,* Golembiewski and Blumberg (Eds.), pp. 349-352.

9. Merle M. Ohlsen, *Group Counseling,* pp. 193-239.

10. Helen I. Driver, *Counseling and Learning through Small-Group Discussion,* p. 167 ff.

11. S. B. Morris, J. Pflugrath, and B. Taylor, "Encounter in Higher Education," in Burton, *Encounter,* pp. 192-93.

12. George B. Leonard, *Education and Ecstasy,* p. 16.

13. This is Terry Borton's description of the way schools can become by stressing the process of coping with a student's real concerns. *Reach, Touch, and Teach,* p. vii.

14. Robert C. Leslie, *Sharing Groups in the Church,* p. 7.

15. George Webber, *The Congregation in Mission.* Nashville: Abingdon Press, 1964, pp. 116-17.

16. James Bugental (Ed.), *The Challenges of Humanistic Psychology,* New York: McGraw-Hill, 1967, p. vii.

17. For a discussion of the relation of existential anxiety to religion, see Clinebell, *Basic Types of Pastoral Counseling,* Chap. 14.

18. Robert A. Raines, *New Life in the Church,* New York: Harper & Row, 1961.

19. Haciendia Heights, Calif., United Church of Christ; Ralph Earle was the pastor.

20. David H. Plate, "Encouraging Growth Groups," *The Christian Advocate,* August 22, 1968.

21. Letter from Vernon L. Story, June 7, 1970.

22. Letter from Arthur C. Morgan, April 20, 1970; Kenneth Jones was the minister in charge of group development.

23. Letter from Reilly N. Hook, May 25, 1971.

24. "Group Psychotherapy and Group Methods in Community Mental Health Programs," a report presented at the 25th and 26th annual meetings of the American Group Psychotherapy Assn., 1969-70.

25. The psychologist is Lawrence D. Mathae.

26. Letter from Oakley Dyer, June 7, 1971.

27. Letter from Joan Macy, FSA, Riverside, Calif., May 19, 1971.

28. Golembiewski and Blumberg (Eds.), *Sensitivity Training and the Laboratory Approach,* p. 342.

29. Abraham Maslow, *Eupsychian Management,* pp. 17-33, 88-107.

30. See Erikson, "Identity and the Life Cycle," *Psychological Issues,* Vol. 1, No. 1 1959, for a fuller discussion of the stages. The chart is adapted from two charts developed by task forces in my seminar, "Group Counseling in the Church." I am indebted to these groups.

CHAPTER 10

Training Change Agents to Humanize Society (With Special Emphasis on Ecology)

Every step toward the goal of justice requires sacrifice, suffering, and struggle; the tireless exertions and passionate concern of dedicated individuals.

A great revolution is taking place in our world, a social revolution in the minds and souls of men. And it has been transformed into a unified voice, crying out, "We want to be free."

MARTIN LUTHER KING[1]

ENTHUSIASM FOR GROWTH GROUPS and their philosophy of self-actualization can dull awareness of the need to eliminate social evils. It can diminish a sense of *social* responsibility precisely because the goal—individual growth—*is* so important. But, if enthusiasm for individual-actualization is misused as an excuse for privitism, the long-range results will be growth-stifling for everyone on the planet.

Releasing the people dynamic in individuals, awakening un-used potentialities, and enlivening intimate relationships are all tremendously important—but not the total task. For while this is being accomplished with ten people, a thousand will have their dreams of a full life mangled by racism, poverty, pollution, social injustice, political tyranny, and the population crush. Individual growth is short-lived unless institutional changes undergird personal change. We must work to produce personal growth that will energize social change, and social change that will nurture and support personal growth.

The new life-power produced in groups must be hooked to action for social change. Growth groups need not be used as psychological fiddling while the world burns. They can contribute to a people-serving society by generating a robust sense of social responsibility. Because they can combine growth and action objectives, growth groups constitute a major resource for social change.

A UNIFIED MODEL OF GROWTH-CHANGE

Here is a unified model of the interrelated spheres of activity of growth and change agents.

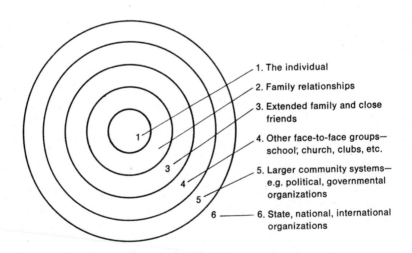

1. The individual
2. Family relationships
3. Extended family and close friends
4. Other face-to-face groups—school, church, clubs, etc.
5. Larger community systems—e.g. political, governmental organizations
6. State, national, international organizations

Which change/growth methods are useful in each sphere of this target? Education, counseling, psychotherapy, and growth groups can produce change in individuals (circle 1). Relationship-oriented counseling methods (couple marriage counseling, family therapy) and growth groups are viable instruments of change within the intimate relationships of circle 2. In circle 3 (the supportive relationships just beyond the family) and circle 4 (other small groups), dynamic education, group therapy, and growth groups are effective methods. Changes in circle 5 (larger, more impersonal organizations) and circle 6 (the systems beyond the local community) may occur through educational persuasive approaches, but often they require the use of political methods.

Personal growth, we have seen, occurs in relationships where there is both *caring* (acceptance, relatedness) and *confrontation* (with reality, the consequences of one's behavior, etc.). All change activity involves varying ratios of these two elements. Growth groups aimed at holding these in even balance are effective in the smaller systems (circles 1 through 4). Effecting change in larger systems (circles 5 and 6) and between systems usually involves a greater use of confrontation in the form of political and economic power.

Any social system, by definition, is more than the sum of its parts. Families, groups, and organizations have identities and internal dynamics which mark them as unique social organisms. Operating in such organisms are forces (called "group dynamics") which are more than a composite of the forces motivating individual members. To improve institutions, methods which take these dynamics into account must be used. Change within any system depends on interaction with other systems. On the target of systems (above), *change in one circle is more likely to occur and be permanent if the systems on one or both sides also change.* To illustrate, individual growth is more likely to occur and be sustained if the family also changes constructively; family changes are more likely to occur and be sustained if the extended family changes to support them; growth in all three is more likely to occur and be sustained if the institutions of society are growth-oriented. Movement toward a person-enhancing world community requires simultaneous action for change in each sphere on the target.

GROWTH GROUPS: INSTRUMENTS OF SOCIAL CHANGE

Social change activities aim at improving our institutions so they will serve our needs more fully. John Gardner, former head of the U.S. Department of Health, Education, and Welfare, states the challenge: "The true task is to design a society (and institutions) capable of continuous change, continuous renewal, continuous responsiveness to human need."[2] In creating such a need-satisfying society, growth groups play an important role.

The process of social change includes five steps.[3] Here are some ways growth groups can help implement these:

Step 1: *Recruitment and Training of an Action Task Force*— The most efficient instrument for social change is a trained action group with a realistic and specific change target. To change any organization requires team effort. Growth group methods are useful in training the team.

(a) *Awakening awareness of the need for action:* Team members are more likely to persist when the going gets rough if they are motivated by an awareness of the suffering caused by the injustice they are fighting. Firsthand confrontation with the victims of social and economic oppression can awaken this crucial awareness.

"Project Understanding" was a two-year effort by teams of theological students, laymen, and clergymen to devise methods for reducing White racism in suburban congregations.[4] The training of participants included plunges into the inner city and encounters with Black and Brown rage. The deeply personal learnings which resulted came from confrontations with the victims of social exploitation and from the debriefing in small rap sessions. Important insights included an awareness of the depth of pain and anger of ghetto residents and the realization that the political and economic keys to the ghetto "prisons" are usually held by white hands in the suburbs.

This model of learning is the experience-reflection-conceptualization-action approach. Beginning with the swirl of feelings, ideas, and impressions from the encounter, the small group encourages critical reflection and sharing of feelings; this may lead to the discovery of principles and action-goals implicit in the experience. Without the growth group, anxiety from direct encounters with injustice-bred rage often produces defensiveness rather than openness to new understanding.

An important aspect of growth which groups can facilitate is an awareness of one's own hidden prejudices. A training group of Caucasian clergymen and mental health professionals used this awareness exercise:

Close your eyes so that you can be more aware of your experiences. Imagine a movie screen within your mind. On it picture yourself looking in a mirror . . . Now picture yourself getting into bed and going to sleep . . . Now you are getting up and walking to the mirror. As you look at yourself, you suddenly realize that your face has changed to that of a Negro . . . How do you feel as a Black? . . . how does your family feel? . . . the person who's planning to marry your son or daughter? . . . Picture yourself going to work . . . having friends over . . . buying a house . . . Now, picture yourself going to bed again and falling asleep . . . Now you are getting up . . . looking in the mirror. You discover that your face is that of a White person again. How do you feel about this change? ·

Debriefing revealed that many of the participants had become aware of race-related feelings—shock, fear, expectation of rejection, vulnerability, confusion, inferiority as a Black, relief at being White again, and guilt about these responses.[5] This group was relatively free of conscious prejudices and was dedicated to racial justice. Yet if their hidden feelings had not been discovered and dealt with, they could have sabotaged their best efforts at social change.

This exercise is useful for gaining awareness of other attitudinal blind spots:

In a male/female liberation group: "See yourself in the mirror as a member of the opposite sex . . ."

In an interfaith group: "See yourself as a Catholic, etc."

In a middle-class group: "See yourself as a lifelong welfare recipient . . ."

In a training-for-caring group: "See yourself as terminally ill . . ."

In an all-Christian group: "See yourself as a Jew . . ." (Hindu, atheist)

These self-confrontations through fantasy offer opportunities for changing relationship-damaging attitudes through group interaction. The world of many people is one of walls without windows. This approach opens windows of communication through the walls *within* and *between* us.

(b) *Equipping change agents with skills:* Social actionists often stumble over their own ineptness in communication and relationships, and their ambivalence about risk-taking and aggressiveness.

Training action teams for Project Understanding began with an intensive weekend at a mountain camp, utilizing a combination of growth groups and communication exercises. The purpose was to increase depth-relating and honest confrontation among the trainees and to provide a model of how to use small groups as instruments of change in churches. *Educative-persuasive* change methods were emphasized. (Subsequent training at the urban action center focused on *negotiation* and *conflict* models of social change, involving the constructive uses of bargaining, political and economic power.)

The training in interpersonal skills sought to enhance these characteristics, seen as necessary for effective social action: the ability to *risk* (stick one's neck out), *use one's aggressiveness* appropriately (not be helpless), *take responsibility* (not pass the buck), *work in team problem-solving* (not be a lone operator), *communicate* clearly and with punch, *establish a connection* with others, *listen* to what others are saying and feeling, *be action- as well as reflection-oriented*, and *deal constructively with interpersonal conflict*. In the training, gaming or simulation of a conflict between subgroups introduced the trainees to intergroup problems in social change.

Interpersonal skill training in growth groups is only part of preparation for effective social action. It is, however, an essential and often-neglected part.*

(c) *Team Building:* To work together efficiently, an action task force needs a sturdy sense of mutual openness and trust. A sense of solidarity is essential when the flack begins to fly—from vested interests which resist changes threatening to their privileges. Awareness and communication exercises in the early phases of an action-growth group are useful in team-building. Both interpersonal relationship marathons and urban "plunges" (a weekend in the ghetto) increase group cohesiveness dramatically in training laymen for social action. An action group should operate with person-respecting methods so that it contributes to its members' growth as it accomplishes its social change objectives. Shared decision-making, collaborative planning, frequent evaluation, and replanning based on this feedback are examples of such methods.

Training groups in twenty-eight churches constituted "Project Laity," designed to help laymen become more involved in the structures and decisions of their communities. The twelve groups

---

* Because of the overlapping of skills required in personal caring and in social action, it is productive to train persons for both activities in the same groups. This was one finding of a pilot project involving fifteen lay training groups. (The project was funded by the W. Clement and Jessie V. Stone Foundation at the School of Theology, Claremont, Calif. 1970-71.)

which completed training demonstrated that "the development of trust emerges from the confrontation of conflict" within the group.[6] Groups which avoided facing their internal conflict developed much less intimacy and trust. Only where trust developed did groups engage in significant social action. Without such a base, it is almost impossible for most individuals even to conceive of themselves as potentially effective in solving social problems. Participants in the twelve groups completing the training pointed to *personal growth*—resulting from freedom of communication, self-expression, and mutual support—as the major satisfaction they derived.

Step 2: *Understanding the problem and deciding on action goals.* Obtaining and interpreting information about social problems are essential aspects of social change in which the small group should be involved. Collecting information often involves direct exposure to problems; this tends to reinforce motivation to take constructive action. One social action group in New York, as a result of the shocking facts about living conditions learned during a door-to-door survey in a slum area, became "fired up" about the need for low-cost housing. Understanding complex social problems (including resources and resistance to change) is best achieved by utilizing the group's total brain-power and experience in subcommittees with specific tasks. As understanding emerges in the group process, alternative action goals will become apparent. Decision-making about *which* goal(s) to implement should involve the whole group; otherwise it is unlikely that participants will support the action with gut-level commitment. If a project is to "fly," differences of opinion among task force members must be faced and discussed openly until areas of agreement are found.

Step 3: *Formulating action strategy.* Decisions about how to accomplish the goals, how to use resources, acquire allies, and divide responsibilities should also be made via the group process.

Everyone must know that his views are valued by the group and that he is "in" on *developing* the plans he will be asked to implement. Growth in the ability to work as a team toward shared goals occurs as the group uses person-respecting methods at each stage.

Step 4: *Action.* During the action phase, it is important to maintain open communication among task force members so that misunderstandings, duplication of efforts, and working at cross-purposes will not impede effectiveness. Frequent opportunities to communicate and resolve conflicts within the team are essential.

When social-change goals involve building bridges between estranged groups, confrontation methods are useful. Racial confrontation groups have been used widely by schools, churches, and police departments. Several high schools in Portland sponsored three interracial encounter weekends at a center overlooking the Columbia River. Led by a psychologist, the youth, teachers, and graduate students spent most of the weekends in confrontation groups of fifteen. Various trust and communication exercises were used. According to reports from the schools, the aim of the project—to reduce racial tensions by building trust and communication—seemed to have been realized.

A twenty-four-hour confrontation marathon was co-led by Price Cobbs and George Leonard for fourteen persons including a White policeman, a Black welfare mother, a Black Vietnam veteran, a well-to-do White matron, and a Black Panther. The early hours were dominated by the Blacks, demanding honesty from each other—"getting the brothers together."

To get the whites together . . . to get them out of the armor built by lifetimes of rationalization is not so easy. We spent hours working with a young white liberal. He starts out very Christian, full of love for all humanity. . . . The blacks don't trust his bland assurances; they sense he has no access to his real feelings. We all stay with him, digging for a level of reality beneath that iron-plated, liberal-Christian armor. At last, we are all with him as he shouts his hatred at every black in the room, at some of the whites. The sound rises in Wagnerian crescendo. It is frightening, wildly hilarious, and somehow liberating. The sound deafens, but it is a better sound than sirens and riot guns. It is the sound of truth, a rare thing these days.[7]

There was no attempt to "integrate" the group. "Let the blacks get blacker, the whites whiter, the browns browner. Let every man be himself in full." When this occurs and the group has gone *through* the anger and denunciation, a spontaneous outpouring of love follows. A Black Panther pins his "I'm Black and Proud" button on a White doctor (who had shown an unusual amount of soul), proclaiming him an "honorary nigger." Application of learnings outside the group is stressed: "If something is learned, if a heart is changed, we urge the change be reflected on the job, in the community, in politics."

The target picked by one Project Understanding team was developing racial understanding and awareness in elementary education in two suburban school districts. In-service training series for teachers (with academic credit from a state university) were held; these included:

Part 1—*Racial Awareness Exposure,* which consisted of a Friday night/ Saturday plunge-encounter in the minority community.
Part 2—*New White Consciousness Seminar* (15 ½ hours) using simulation, small group interaction, and lectures to cultivate new perspectives on White identity gained from the exposure.
Part 3—A four-hour *Follow-Up Workshop* held in the schools where the teachers work—for evaluation and further applications of learnings to their job problems.

This approach awakens awareness of the problems faced by minorities and nurtures the emergence of a person-respecting White identity based on self-esteem.[8]

Growth groups are also useful for *interrupting the vicious cycle* *of individual and social problems.* Project ENABLE* trained some two hundred indigenous nonprofessionals and two hundred professionals in group family life education and neighborhood action methods for use with low-income families. The goal was to eliminate the effects of chronic poverty on families—effects which tend to perpetuate the poverty cycle. Some eight hundred parents' groups were established in sixty-two communities, involving fifteen thousand low-income parents. Discussion in the parents' groups centered on their children, community facilities, their own adequacy as parents, how to communicate with their children, control their own emotions in handling them, and raise them to be law-abiding citizens. Project ENABLE helped families learn how to take initiative and make decisions in matters affecting their welfare. The parents worked together on some three hundred neighborhood improvement projects aimed at getting better housing, recreational facilities, police protection, health care, and closer relations with schools and welfare programs. This project shows that personal growth and social action objectives must be integrated in groups designed to help persons extricate themselves from the web of chronic poverty. It demonstrates that "poor families can be helped to overcome isolation and despair by solving difficult family and community problems together."[9]

Step 5: *Evaluation and restrategizing.* Social action teams should evaluate their goals/strategies/actions with the openness and honesty which characterize growth groups. Maximum learning from both successes and failures occurs in such an atmosphere. Reformulation of goals and restrategizing develop out of the group evaluative process.

The action training center in a Pacific Northwest city sponsored a series of courses on strategies for urban social action. Several task

* Education and Neighborhood Action for Better Living Environment.

groups evolved from these; their goal was to raise the level of concern on the city council by working to elect candidates aware of urban problems. After the election (in which the goals were largely achieved), the action training center sponsored a "weekend away" for those who had been intensely involved. The objectives were to reflect on the recent election, decide what goals to seek next, plan strategy, and replenish energies for the new effort.

INTERGROUP POLARIZATION AND COMMUNICATION

Social change often involves conflicts and communication problems between various groups, each with its own identity, values, commitments, goals, and power dynamics. It is essential, therefore, to be aware of the dynamics of intergroup conflict. The following communication exercise can be productive in the training or the action steps of social change. It is effective with any two groups committed to contrasting values. Here is how it is used in training adult leaders for youth growth groups.

The training group is divided in half; those on one side are told:

"Whatever your actual age, for this exercise you are part of the youth counter culture. You have long hair, beads and bare feet. You believe passionately in the things these youth see as important. Review these values in your mind and recall how young people feel about them. Let yourself move inside their world; feel the way they feel."

Those on the other side are told:

"Whatever your actual age, for this experience you are part of middle America. You've over forty and can remember the great depression. You are involved in the institutions of your community. You feel strongly that the basic values of our society are important and must be preserved. You carry heavy responsibilities—on your job, in the community, and in coping with being middle aged and parents of teen-agers. Think about the things that are most important to you and how you feel about them."

After a pause to let each side get inside the roles, the leader says: "I invite you to turn your chairs toward the other group . . . Now will you adults tell these young people the things that really matter to you." As the "adults" talk to the "youth," the leader lists the values they mention (on newsprint or a blackboard). If the "youth" are in their roles, they'll take only a few minutes of what usually registers as condescending, self-righteous adult pronouncements. If they don't begin to talk back spontaneously, after a few minutes, the leader invites them to "tell these adults how it is as you see it." The "youth" values are listed beside those of the "adults."

The temperature of the exchange usually soars. Before long, each side is "lobbing hand grenades," as one participant put it. After the polarization has increased and the verbal battle has escalated, the leader interrupts, asking those on either side how they are feeling. Frequently present are anger at not being heard or understood, alienation, and the impulse to attack more vigorously.

After debriefing, the sides are reversed. The leader describes the two roles again, and the exchange about "what's really important" continues, usually with polarization in reverse. After awhile this phase is debriefed thoroughly. The anger level is lowered as the process is discussed. Then the leader asks: "Are there other ways to communicate—ways that might result in more messages getting through?" Back in their second roles, group members try to build bridges rather than barriers. Coaching from the leader may be necessary—e.g., "Try stating how *you* feel . . . without making a disguised attack." or "Could you let the other side know you hear what they're saying?" Continue until some success in connecting across the youth-adult communication chasm is achieved.*

This exercise is useful in adult and youth workshops and in adult-youth growth groups. When the two groups are actually present, skilled facilitators are needed to coach both sides in communication skills. Take plenty of time to work through and learn from the rich, powerful feelings stirred up by this exercise. Whenever possible, the technique should be employed at the start of a several-day laboratory session in conflict-resolution or communication so that the groups can move beyond polarization.

Here are some learning-growth experiences which emerge from this process: (1) The group experiences the value-gulf alienating two conflicting groups. (2) It participates in the powerful experience of group polarization and the kinds of communication which produce it—e.g., attacking, not listening, "telling" the other side, we're-right-you're-wrong messages, etc. (3) The role reversal develops awareness of the important values on both sides of the gulf and awareness of one's own ambivalence regarding the two value worlds. (4) Participants can discover and practice styles of communication that reduce polarization and increase understanding—owning and expressing one's own needs rather than trying to convert the other, listening with understanding, etc. (5) If the group learns these bridge-building skills, it can break out of the win-lose struggle and achieve a degree of difference-respecting, collaborative intergroup relationships.

MOTIVATING ADULTS TO ACTION

Without glamorizing the motives of youth, it is important to recognize that many young people have awakened to pro-people values and life-styles which can have a salutary influence on our

---

* Dividing "youth" and "adults" into mixed groups of four to six, during part of this exercise, lets them experience the striking differences between larger group-to-group and more intimate person-to-person communication.

society. Depth youth-adult encounters in small groups may help create a society that weds the viable from the past with new humanizing relationships and institutions.

Joseph Fletcher observes that although the "compassion quotient" of most adults in our bourgeois culture is low, they do care intensely about their children—who in turn care intensely about poverty, racism, ecology, and war.[10] He sees this as a potential lever to motivate adults to become involved in desperately needed social action. I would add that transgenerational confrontation/communication groups can help develop shared commitments to values and action which will improve our sick society. There are important values on each side of the generation gap— values which need to be brought together to help persons achieve a full life in a free society.

ECOLOGY GROWTH GROUPS

The need for groups with a dual focus on personal growth and social change is illustrated by the crisis in our environment. Reflect for a moment on a few familiar facts: The endangered wildlife list now stands at a record 101 species in the United States —mammals, birds, fish, amphibians, and reptiles facing extinction. Each year we spew 183 million tons of contaminants into our fragile envelope of air. Many of our rivers are open sewers. Each week the world has 1,396,000 new mouths to feed, a large proportion in the poorer nations. Almost half of the world's 3.6 billion human beings are undernourished or malnourished. By 1985, if noise pollution trends continue, people more than two feet apart on an average urban street corner will have to scream to be heard. One student of the current scene states: "We seem to be quite capable of polluting ourselves out of meaningful existence. All we have to do is to continue with our most thoughtless present practices."[11] It's frighteningly obvious to thoughtful persons that the human race—equipped with the bomb, the engine, and other fruits of technology; with arrogant disregard for nature and for other animals; and with a tragically immature social conscience—is itself on the endangered species list.

The delicate balance among and between all living things and their environment (the ecosystem) has been upset by man, particularly affluent western man with his technology and resource-gobbling living standard. (An average American uses up natural resources at a rate fifty times greater than that of an average person in India.) If we care at all about the kind of world in which our children and grandchildren will live, our values, relations with nature, and destructive life-styles must be drastically reoriented. We can no longer ignore the fact that we are part of the delicate balance of living things. The quality of our lives will depend increasingly on respecting this profound fact.

Growth-action groups can help us simultaneously develop sensitive ecological consciences and carry out social action to save the environment on which all life depends. As Arnold Toynbee once said, "The necessary condition for making technology bear fruit that will be sweet and not bitter is a spiritual change of heart. . . ."[12] Such a change of heart is the goal of dynamic ecology education which must have high priority in schools, families, and churches. Three dimensions of growth are necessary in this process: *comprehension* of the crisis, *conversion* of our attitudes, and *commitment* of our consciences and behavior. The crisis is a struggle for survival; this can best be comprehended in study-action groups. Within these groups, attitudes toward nature can be transformed—from arrogant, exploitative domination to respectful affinity with the natural world. Such change requires experiencing our organic bond with nature—with the air, the ocean, and the earth; with all living things; and with the world-wide human family. In the words of the priest-scientist Teilhard de Chardin:

The world . . . to which we brought the boredom and callousness reserved for profane places, is in truth a holy place . . . Venite, adoremus.[13]

Commitment of our consciences means implementing life-respecting attitudes by earthy actions such as recycling wastes, reducing our greedy consumption of natural resources, and engaging in group efforts (e.g., economic boycotts and political action) to achieve practical ecological objectives.

Ecology awareness-action groups can help us, in Ralph Waldo Emerson's words, to "enjoy an original relation to the universe."[14] Perhaps you recall precious moments—when you have been aware of such a relationship. I remember lying on the warm glacier-polished granite high on a mountain and feeling a strange connection between the rock and a primitive something in me. Or the moving moment of finding a fossil seashell near a peak in the Rockies more than 10,000 feet above the sea. Or the sunny day in spring when the growth forces all around in our garden seemed somehow to be flowing also through me. Discovering and renewing one's inner ties with nature are essential to maintaining enthusiasm for the ecological struggle. Lifelong love affairs with nature can be sparked by experiencing it with someone who is sensitive, informed, and alive to the wonders of the universe.

Sensitizing our individual consciences ecologically and practicing respect for the environment are essential starting places. But it is crucial to move beyond these to joint political action. In the long run only more enlightened laws and public policies can bring victory in the struggle. Local groups should ally themselves with the national ecology groups which are educationally and politically effective.

Every community has its pollution and ecology problems. A lay training-for-mission group in a Protestant church[15] began by listening to their community and its needs. They decided that they "must work toward creating an ecological conscience in this church, community, and beyond." A sensitive physicist took them on a hike in the nearby mountains to experience "the livingness of nature which we seek to preserve." They read extensively and discussed the material. They related what they learned to their group's guiding beliefs—by discovering biblical and theological foundations for good ecology. Their group-created strategy included these actions: establishing cooperative links with other churches and groups committed to ecology; developing a Center of Ecology Information and a paperback book table at the church; devising methods to reach decision-makers in the community; exploring the development of a coordinating council of all ecology groups active in that community—Sierra Club, Friends of the Earth, Zero Population Growth, League of Conservation Voters, Wilderness Society, National Wildlife Federation, National Audubon Society, World Population, GASP (Group Against Smog Pollution), Planned Parenthood, etc. This group used an integrated growth-action approach working at both ends of the ecological crisis—personal growth through a broad educational thrust and social change through community action.

ECOLOGY AND THE GOOD LIFE

The ecological perspective provides a wide-angle lens for viewing the human potentials situation on our planet. As biologists Paul and Anne Ehrlich make clear,[16] the diverse problems humanity faces—overpopulation, war, widespread hunger, pollution, resource depletion—all intertwine. Collectively they pose an unprecedented threat and challenge to all mankind. Unless the population explosion can be controlled, all measures to save the environment will be exercises in futility. Growth-action groups can make a small but significant contribution to defusing the "population bomb" at the personal level. Couples can discover ways to satisfy their needs for security, self-esteem and creativity other than by having many children. On a social action level, groups can work for objectives such as income tax incentives to reward small rather than large families and freely available family planning resources for everyone everywhere.

The ultimate pollutant is, of course, war. Until the monster weapons of the nuclear powers are controlled by world structures of peace and justice, mankind flirts daily with extinction. I recall a moving conversation with a Greek population biologist (whom I encountered on a recent plane trip). Commenting on the importance of the rising tide of respect for the environment, he observed: "But all our efforts in the ecology fight will be wasted unless we prevent the war that will pollute the whole earth in a day." I'm not claiming that a network of growth groups by itself will prevent a nuclear doomsday. But it can help by reducing the enormous reservoir of individual anger, frustration, and unlived life that fuels collective hostilities. Growth groups can help more and more of us increase our ability to live and to love. Loving people will support movements and leaders who are tuned to the people dynamic. Loving people, who are also politically skilled, can elect leaders who are genuine statesmen and peacemakers. Loving, open, growing people are best prepared to function as citizens of the world community with ultimate commitment to the human race.

Growth groups can also be used to build bridges of communication and empathy across the barriers that divide mankind— the ethnic, racial, national, and political differences that isolate us from our fellow human beings, During several workshops on counseling in India, my wife and I led growth groups for participants. In spite of the vast differences in languages and cultures among group members and between them and us as leaders, remarkable things happened. We discovered that it was possible, in many cases, to transcend barriers of culture and *touch each other's common humanity*. That these groups (in what we had feared would be an unpromising setting) had an impact was clear in the responses of many participants. In the closing group evaluation period, one Indian priest said to a fellow priest, "We have been living, studying, and eating together in the same small seminary for nine years, yet I feel I've come to know you better in this group than in all that time."

The discovery that growth groups can be effective in another culture, even when led by "outsiders," strengthened our appreciation of the extraordinary power, usefulness, and adaptability of this method. It reinforced our belief that a significant contribution to world peace could be made by the widespread use of intercultural and international growth groups.

In the earlier chapters of this book, the thrust was on the development of the full potential of individuals in caring communities called growth groups. Individuals can develop their potentialities only as they experience a mutual fulfillment with other people. This can happen fully only as organizations and social structures support the life-style of personal growth. Thus, personal growth and social growth need each other. Furthermore, in finding one's cause and pouring oneself into it, a dimension of new growth becomes available. To paraphrase the words of a first-century carpenter: "A person who hoards his life will only exist, but one who invests himself gladly in efforts to create a better world will find the secret of life in its fullness."

For millions of us earthlings, the pictures of earth from thousands of miles in space give a fresh perspective on our human situation. Archibald MacLeish described it in these beautiful and now-familiar words:

To see the earth as it truly is, small and blue and beautiful in that eternal silence where it floats, is to see ourselves as riders on the earth together, brothers on that bright loveliness in the eternal cold—brothers who know now that they are truly brothers.[17]

Looking back toward the earth from near the moon, one space-man declared wistfully, "It looks like a good place to live." In these words he expressed both a present truth and a challenge for the future. That's our task, humanizing our society—economi-cally, politically, interpersonally, religiously, environmentally—so that it will be, in fact, a good place for everyone. Finding your unique role in helping to create a world society dedicated to human fulfillment can open a new chapter in your personal jour-ney toward wholeness.

The "greening of America," of western society, of the world community, can only occur as we develop a generally available network of opportunities for experiencing the people dynamic—the power of people to create and recreate themselves and each other in intimate relationships. The lethal destructiveness that erupts in a thousand forms of violence around the globe stems from the anger of loneliness, the guilt of massive unlived life, the despair of ever getting one's physical and emotional needs satisfied. Growth groups, in their many forms, offer a promising strategy for ending the tragic waste of our most important re-source—people. They are our best hope for using the *people dynamic* to create a more *dynamic people* throughout the earth.

Additional Reading—Training Change Agents

SOCIAL CHANGE:

Bennett, Thomas R., II, *The Leader and the Process of Change.* New York: Association Press, 1962.

Bennis, Warren; Benne, Kenneth; and Chin, Robert (Eds.), *The Plan-ning of Change.* New York: Holt, Rinehart and Winston, 1961.

Bonthius, Robert H., "Training Clergymen to Change Community Structures," in *Community Mental Health, The Role of Church and Temple,* H. J. Clinebell, Jr. (Ed.). Nashville: Abingdon Press, 1970. pp. 41 ff.

Brody, Ralph and Cremer, Kay, *Organizing for Social Change, A Case Study Approach.* Cleveland: Cleveland State University, 1970.

Lippitt, Ronald; Watson, Jeanne; and Westley, Bruce, *The Dynamics of Planned Change*. New York: Harcourt, Brace and World, 1958.

Sanford, Nevitt, *Self and Society, Social Change and Individual Development*. New York: Atherton Press, 1966.

Schein, E. and Bennis, W., *Personal and Organizational Change Through Group Methods*. New York: Wiley, 1965.

Seifert, Harvey, and Clinebell, H. J., Jr., *Personal Growth and Social Change*. Philadelphia: Westminster Press, 1969. A guide for ministers and laymen as change agents.

ECOLOGY:

Ehrlich, Paul R. and Anne H., *Population, Resources, Environment: Issues in Human Ecology*. San Francisco: W. H. Freeman and Co., 1970.

Eiseley, Loren C., *The Immense Journey*. New York: Random House, 1957.

IDOC, "A Theology of Survival," September, 1970.

Imsland, Donald, *Celebrate the Earth*. Minneapolis: Augsburg Publishing House, 1971.

Johnson, Huey (Ed.), *No Deposit-No Return, Man and His Environment: A View Toward Survival*. Reading, Mass.: Addison-Wesley Publishing Co., 1970.

Rienow, Robert and Leona, *Moment in the Sun*. New York: Ballantine Books, 1967.

Udall, Stewart L., *The Quiet Crisis*. New York: Holt, Rinehart, and Winston, 1963.

REFERENCES

1. *The Wisdom of Martin Luther King*, edited by the staff of Bill Adler Books (New York: Lancer Books, 1968), pp. 85, 99.

2. Sumner B. Norris, *et al.*, "Encounter in Higher Education," in Burton *Encounter*, pp. 200-201.

3. For a more detailed discussion of these phases of change, see Harvey Seifert and H. J. Clinebell, Jr., *Personal Growth and Social Change*, Chap. 4, "The Process of Growth and Change."

4. This project was funded by the Irwin-Sweeny-Miller Foundation through the School of Theology at Claremont, Calif.

5. In another workshop one participant reported that he was touched

powerfully by this experience, "finding a dislike of black skin and feelings of white superiority that I really didn't think I had."

6. Thomas R. Bennett II, "Project Laity: Groups and Social Action," *The Creative Role of Interpersonal Groups in the Church Today*, John Casteel (Ed.), p. 66.

7. George B. Leonard, "How to Have a Bloodless Riot," *Look*, June 10, 1969, p. 26. The other two quotes are from p. 28 and p. 25. In their racial confrontation groups Cobbs and Leonard have not discovered a Black who isn't angry or a White who isn't prejudiced.

8. This series was developed by Bill Johnson and Caddy Jackson, of the School of Theology at Claremont, working with the education task force of Project Understanding in the San Diego area.

9. "The Business Community Has No Higher Priority . . . Than Strengthening of Family Life," FSAA, 1968, p. 24. See also *Family Service Highlights*, Sept./Nov., 1965, pp. 26-27.

10. "Generation Gap: Opportunity Lever," *The Churchman*, Aug./Sept., 1970, p. 6.

11. John A. Day, "Ecosystem: Key Word for the 70's," *Faculty Forum*, March, 1970, p. 1.

12. *The Churchman*, March, 1969 (Cover).

13. *The Divine Milieu*, New York: Harper & Row, 1960, p. 89.

14. Stewart Udall, *The Quiet Crisis* (New York: Avon Books, 1964), p. 55.

15. Good Shepherd Lutheran Church, Claremont, Calif.; Sam Emerick, Director of the Yokefellow Center in Indiana, led the group.

16. Ehrlich and Ehrlich, *Population, Resources, Environment*.

17. Imsland, *Celebrate the Earth*, p. 41.

Index

74 75 10 9 8 7 6 5 4 3